Improvisation for Actors and Writers

A guidebook for improv lessons in comedy

Bill Lynn

Foreword by Kip King, The Groundlings Theatre

MERIWETHER PUBLISHING LTD.
Colorado Springs, Colorado

Meriwether Publishing Ltd., Publisher
PO Box 7710
Colorado Springs, CO 80933-7710

Editor: Arthur Zapel
Editorial assistant: Dianne Bundt
Cover design: Jan Melvin

© Copyright MMIV Meriwether Publishing Ltd.
Printed in the United States of America
First Edition

Library of Congress Cataloging-in-Publication Data

Lynn, Bill, 1964-
    Improvisation for actors and writers : a guidebook for improv lessons in comedy / Bill Lynn ; foreword by Kip King.
        p. cm.
    Includes index.
    ISBN 1-56608-094-0
1. Improvisation (Acting) 2. Comedy--Authorship. 3. Stand-up comedy. I. Title.
    PN2071.I5L96 2004
    792.02'8--dc22

                                2003027766

        1   2   3   4   04   05   06

Dedication
To Bridget, Jimmy, and Mom

Acknowledgments

Kip King, Stan Wells, Patrick Bristow, Charna Halpern,
Cathy Shambley, Ted Michaels, Phyllis Katz,
Amy Von Freymann, Maggie Baird, Cherie Kerr, Natalie Skelton,
Cooper Thornton, Adam Katz, Brooke Cadorette, Marie Petite,
Maria Quinones, Eileen Dulen Jennings,
Connie Calderon, Marty Madden, Peg Hey,
Loretta Shenosky, Sven Lindstrom, Tom Tangen,
Duncan and Lilli Rouleau, James Adomian,
John and MaryAnn Ahart

Contents

Foreword

Some students today are result-oriented. They go for the result without doing the work. It's almost like an Olympic runner who hitchhikes: "Can you give me a ride to the finish line here? I gotta be faster than everybody else." You cannot trade off. You have to do the work step by step yourself.

And the place to start is *inside*.

At first, I didn't think I could teach improvisation. One particular time, a Groundling teacher had to cancel right before my class. I started to panic. The teacher said, "You teach it." I answered, "I don't know what to do!" I was shaking in my boots. I was frightened to death. But I had to teach improv, so I taught improv.

Later, I developed a character in The Groundlings, a character named Brendan O'Phlegm, a pompous Irish improv instructor:

Improvisation is makin' it up as ya go along! Doin' what ya damn well please! (To the audience) How are ya? (The audience answers "Fine.") You see? Ya made that answer up! Did ya write it down before ya came here? No! That's improvisation, Ladies and Gentlemen!

Audiences loved that character because he was so set in his ways. I lost my inhibitions completely in that character.

You have to be honest with yourself. Things like emptiness and places you want to avoid are actually the places that give you permission to expand. The things we've avoided all our lives are actually the things we need to be drawn to, like a moth to a flame. Those are the places that are unknown, where all your demons come from. You start taming those demons when you *use* them.

But you need to *technically* understand your experiences, and this book is created in order to explain them, describing not the experience itself, but the logistics behind it. You can't just rely on spontaneity — you need the technical in order to explain the spontaneous.

Also, if you place unrealistic demands on yourself, you'll create nothing but discomfort. However, if you take the view that nothing is a mistake, that nothing would happen unless you needed to learn that particular lesson, then eventually you realize that you are actually moving on a specific path — your own individual path (one that you are, quite literally, making up as you go along).

You are realizing your uniqueness as an artist and how to manifest it in your everyday life. It has nothing to do with the competition and all that stuff. When you feel separate, make a connection. Connecting is the goal. Denying the truth never works. You come away feeling like something has been stolen from you. It's really when you lose yourself that you seem to find yourself. So, embrace what's coming at you.

Your path is an unknown path to you. It is made by you, and you alone. *Nobody has ever done "you" before you.* It's important to know that nobody ever, ever did what you're doing right now, the way you're doing it. That cuts out the competition.

So, trust and believe in yourself. Because if you understand yourself, you understand all of humanity. There's no difference — a drop of water, or an ocean.

— Kip King

Kip King is one of the original members of The Groundlings comedy troupe. Kip has appeared in numerous TV shows and films, from *Batman* and *Breakfast at Tiffany's* to *Babylon 5* and *Hollywood Homicide*. He has performed in hundreds of commercials and was the national spokesperson for V8 Juice and Continental Yogurt. He has performed voiceovers for Hanna Barbera, including starring roles in *Smurfs* and *The Biskitts*. He is the father of *Saturday Night Live*'s Chris Kattan and is a renowned acting and improv coach in Los Angeles.

Introduction

Four years ago, I moved to Los Angeles to jump-start my acting career. I attended a variety of improv comedy schools in order to get industry exposure — "stage time," we call it in the acting biz. I showed up thinking that my comedic instincts were all I needed — "I'll just get up there and be funny." I was a company member of a Chicago theater ensemble, I had a degree in theater, some commercial credits, and a few roles in independent short films. I thought it would be easy to become a member of a comedy theater ensemble.

And then I was struck on the head by the proverbial falling anvil.

I realized that as a comedic actor, I was solely responsible for developing my own material. Surprise! It's not just *acting*. It's *writing*. It's developing your own premises, not just for the stage but for film and TV, too. You are the actor, the writer, *and* the producer.

Few of the comedy classes I took had a syllabus, or even a list of class exercises. (Sure, there are books detailing popular improv games, but not a clear documentation of the use of improv to create characters and write sketch comedy.) After I finished the course, I vowed to make it easier for future students. I assembled some exercises common to most schools and developed this road map as a way for students to prepare for what's ahead.

You don't have to be in an improv comedy class to learn from this book. This book is for actors, writers, and comedians — anyone who wants to share their comedic observations.

This book is a student's guide, from a student's perspective. In it you'll find a sample of the basic theories, approaches, exercises, and tips taught in comedy schools around the country, with an eye toward the personal struggle that performers encounter as they delve into comedy for the first time. The sections follow the standard progression of comedy school classes. The first section covers improv schools, the second covers improv basics, the third covers creating characters, the fourth covers long form improv, and the fifth covers sketch writing.

Selected exercise descriptions appear in the text. Additional exercises appear in the appendix. The intent here is to capture the *essence* of the types of exercises you'll encounter in class, not replicate the coursework.

So, use the book as a reference tool to augment your own discovery as you take the classes. It's best if you read only a section or chapter at a time, as you need it. Then come back and review it again later. Comedy is a discipline you'll likely work on for years. It's a layered learning process where you'll discover new applications for old tenets, again and again.

By the time you finish these classes, you'll have a respect for the power of improv, a firm grasp of comedic structure, and the ability to turn your comedic instincts into fully realized *written* premises. You will have laid the groundwork to expand beyond the three-minute medium.

Section 1
Improv Comedy Schools

*"I went to a conservatory theater program in college.
I did tons of comedy. Shakespeare. Simon.
Starlight Express, for God's sake.*

*I mean, what can these people teach me about comedy?
I just want to use this theater to get industry work."*

— Author's Journal, May 2, 2000

Chapter 1

Why Study Improv Comedy?

It's one thing to perform scripted comedy. It's another thing entirely to develop it from scratch. Improv is the best place to start.

Improv creates instant "funny." Because the players make it up as they go along, their ideas collide in the moment, creating inherently flawed situations, capturing the humor of life's incongruities. Improv captures it so well, in fact, that comedy writers use it as a primary creative tool.

Whose Line Is It Anyway, Saturday Night Live (SNL), MadTV, The Simpsons, and films like *Austin Powers* boast writers and actors who have studied improv and sketch comedy at The Groundlings, The Second City, ImprovOlympic, Upright Citizens Brigade, and many other theater schools. The comedy tenets taught at these schools provide students with a sound foundation for developing comedy in any professional medium.

Comedy schools use improv, the art of extemporaneous dramatic action, as the basis for everything — improv for performance, improv for character building, improv for sketch writing, and even improv for developing premises for TV and film. Improv places a dramatic action into a logical, immediate human context. Improv is spontaneous, heightened, flawed, and deeply human.

Most students don't care about that.

Students enroll for a variety of other reasons, depending on their commitment to the art form. Actors take the classes to bolster their on-camera acting skills, or to get industry work. Some take classes just for recreation. The more committed students aspire to become disciplined comedic actors and comedy writers.

Chapter 2

Comedy Schools

The Curriculum

Viola Spolin, the mother of theatrical improv, developed basic theater games for actors in the 1930s. These basic exercises were the initial Big Bang, which spawned or influenced The Second City and the Committee (a San Francisco-based troupe). Later, Spolin published the exercises in her book, *Improvisation for the Theater*.[1] Many other improv comedy groups developed simultaneously, or as offshoots of the initial Big Bang.

Because of the Big Bang, today's improv schools share a series of core exercises steeped in the Viola Spolin tradition. However, in its advanced classes, each school does its own thing, emphasizing a different aspect of comedy performance. Some schools perform improv exclusively, espousing the idea that the art form stands as a medium on its own.

For example, The Second City emphasizes political satire. That is, they emphasize political sketch comedy with social commentary. They also perform short form and long form improv.

The Groundlings emphasizes behavioral satire. That is, their sketch comedy is character-based. In addition, they perform short form and long form improv.

ImprovOlympic focuses on long form improv — namely, the Harold. In addition, they have a level 5B show where students are given the opportunity to perform. They also do sketch shows and reviews and have a writing program. The Empty Stage in west Los Angeles performs long form exclusively, featuring a cast of Emmy Award-winning comedy writers called the Transformers. The

---

[1] For a complete history of improv, I recommend Rob Kozlowski's illuminating work, *The Art of Chicago Improv, Short Cuts to Long-Form Improvisation,* Portsmouth, NJ: Heinemann, 2002.

Upright Citizens Brigade emphasizes long form improv, which they transformed into a sketch format for television in 1998.

Figure 1 shows each school and the type of comedy it champions.

	Short Form Improv	Long Form Improv	Short Scene Sketch Shows	Linked Scene Sketch Shows	Social/Political Satire	Character/Behavioral Satire
The Groundlings	✓	✓	✓		▦	✓
The Second City	✓	✓	✓	✓	✓	▦
ImprovOlympic		✓			✓	
The Empty Stage		✓			✓	
Upright Citizens Brigrade		✓		✓	✓	▦

Figure 1

✓ — Primary Strength
▦ — Secondary Strength

Each institution shares many of the same fundamental improv exercises, and most use improv as a way to build characters and sketch comedy. Each school fiercely prides itself on its respective bailiwick: *short form improv* (extemporized single scenes), *long form improv* (extemporized linked scenes), or *sketch comedy* (written, rehearsed scenes).

The Teachers

The theaters' main stage company members play the role of teacher. They coach students on the tenets of improv, comedy writing, and performance. Many of the teachers are working television and film writers, directors, and actors, some of whom have amassed substantial credentials and industry experience after joining their respective companies.

However, just because your teacher is a working comedian, don't automatically assume he has a great deal of teaching experience. Some improv instructors will snipe and humiliate their classes in order to awaken enlightenment in hard-edged students. Some instructors are so soft in their criticism that their students never really hear the message, and never improve. Remember, the instructors are learning, too.

In the instructors' defense, it's a tough crowd, literally filled with class clowns, so if the instructor is a little harsh, it's understandable. However, the best instructors deliver firm criticism and have polished communication and managerial skills. The best instructors usually teach the upper level classes and quickly rise to the level of director of the main stage show.

The Classes

Typically a program consists of four to five levels of six-week classes, taken in sequence. Depending on waiting lists, it may take up to three years or more to complete the program. There are introductory classes (The Second City has five of these), Fundamental Improv, Intermediate Improv with Characters, Sketch Writing, and Advanced Performance classes, after which the company members may ask you to perform with their "B" company. After performing with their "B" company for six months, they may ask you to join their main stage company.

At the ImprovOlympic, you may perform in a Harold team at the discretion of a committee of teachers. Their decision is based on your performance in a 5B show.

At The Second City, students perform end-of-class shows as they progress through the various classes. When they complete their program, they vie for spots in their various performance companies — from touring companies to main stage shows.

Some company members develop lifelong working relationships. They write, produce, direct, and perform together long after they finish performing in their respective companies.

Chapter 3

Auditioning and Placement

As you prepare for a comedy school audition, you may ask yourself if you're a natural comedian. There are two types of people — those who solve problems, and those who make them worse. If you solve problems, become a producer. If you have the natural predisposition to expose vice and folly, God help you — you're a comedian.

Frankly, these schools' entrance auditions simply attempt to weed out imbalanced or socially maladjusted applicants. On the surface, it appears that comedy welcomes social outcasts. Underneath, however, comedy requires disciplined, well-adjusted communicators.

Because improv relies on your personal experience and instinct, you can't hide who you really are — it all comes rushing out during your improv audition, like it or not. If you're nervous or overly self-conscious, you may resort to blue humor or strange behavior in an effort to prove that you're funny. Avoid this at all costs. Relax and be you. If necessary, get comfortable improvising at a smaller school before auditioning at a larger venue.

Although the number of actor/writer applicants has increased over the years, the schools' requirements have stayed the same: a strong stage presence, some presentation or acting experience, and an expressive, quirky normalcy.

At character-centered comedy schools like The Groundlings, the auditor may ask you to extemporize a monologue as a character with a given attribute.

> **Tip**
>
> Comedy is built on small, logical leaps of absurdity. Be illogical and the audience will abandon you. *"Maurice flew his strawberry airplane over Vatican, Kansas." ("Huh?")*

10

Audition Exercises

Auditions for improv schools vary by instructor and venue. Here is a sampling of audition exercises used at various schools.

One Word Story
(a.k.a., *One Word at a Time* or *Word at a Time Story*)
In this exercise, the group of twelve applicants stands in a circle, and each student, in order, adds one word to build normal sentences that build a logical story. "The ... cat ... walked ... over ... to ... the ... _____." Avoid the temptation to add an odd word like "Louvre" or "clothier" — they're illogical. This is sure to disqualify you. "Food" is probably more normal, or "mouse." Don't try to be funny in this one; this is a test of your logic and normalcy. Just work with your fellow players to tell a *logical* story, one word at a time.

Story/Story,
(a.k.a. *Conducted Story*)
In this audition exercise, five players line up; the director selects a story topic or genre like "Pulp Fiction" or "Romance Novel," and points to a player who starts the story using full sentences. The instructor, like a conductor, points to another player, who must continue the same story just where the previous player left off, seamlessly, mid-sentence or even mid-syllable. Listen to your fellow players. Support their ideas. Avoid adding wild tangents. Stay on course.

"Hello, I'm ..."
(a.k.a. *Superheroes* or *Worst Nightmare*)
In this advanced solo exercise, the instructor selects a player and randomly assigns a superhero title, like "Litigation Man," or "King of Burning Rubber." The instructor asks the player to extemporize a two-minute monologue as that character. The two-minute monologue begins and ends with the identifying phrase, "Yes, I am known as ..." or "Hello, I'm ..." and the player's title. Players use the foundation, who, what, and where.

11

There are key techniques to remember in this exercise. In your dialogue, identify the person to whom your character is talking, play with some imaginary props, have a specific point of view about a specific topic, and stick to it. The more specific your character is about his attitudes and what he is doing, the better. If you're advanced, you'll develop a character with a facade hiding his true feelings. If you're a genius, you'll build in a character theme that is universally human and recognizable to all of us, e.g. (a superhero with a fear of failure or someone who embellishes his own credentials). Exercises like this one are covered in more detail in the section entitled "Developing Comic Characters."

A Simple Three-Person Improv Scene
Some schools only require you to improvise a three-person scene with a given work location, like a Furr's Cafeteria. Instructors can tell if you've studied improvisation before. Can you listen and respond to your partner simply? Do you have a confident stage presence? How much do you know about building a foundation in a scene? Can you grow a premise to a logical conclusion?

Don't fret if you don't pass the audition. Audition again at a later date or go to another school. Most schools offer introductory classes that don't require an audition.

Placement
Generally, most applicants are accepted into these programs and placed in the introductory level. Or, if you're solid enough, you skip the introductory classes and start in the regular series of classes, or the "conservatory." The audition instructor is looking for students who are compliant, composed listeners, comfortable on

stage, and who behave appropriately in a classroom setting. Those candidates who have *good information* (unique ideas that build original scenes) and are familiar with the exercises stand the best chance of being placed in Beginning Improv without having to take any introductory classes.

Chapter 4

What Have I Gotten Myself Into?

The following bits of general advice on comedy classes will help you set your expectations.

The Three-Minute Medium

Improv and sketch comedy scenes usually last only three to five minutes. That's twenty times shorter than a feature film.

This condensed time frame has an impact on the way you improvise and write. You have to set up the exposition more quickly, introduce characters more quickly, and you have to heighten and complete the action. And, if that's not enough, you have to invite the audience to join you in the absurd world of the scene. So, because it's a condensed art form, short form comedy requires extra attention to technique.

Failing Forward

Once you start improvising in class, you'll feel rotten. It's humiliating to be a new improviser because you fail forward, in front of everybody. You learn improv by doing it, making mistakes, receiving instructor notes and trying again.

When your first scenes fail, you will ask yourself some basic questions: "I'm a funny person, but why was I not funny in this improv? Why is this much harder than it looks? Why is the instructor giving me so many notes?"

Improv is different than standup. You must learn improv guidelines in order to be a successful improviser. Improv is a difficult art form, requiring years of practice. Like standup comedy, it only looks easy.

"I'm a Standup. I'll Do Just Fine."

Every professional comedian is funny until he tries to cross over to improv or sketch comedy for the first time. Howard Stern's live

14

awards-show appearance as FartMan, a self-created comic character, fell flat with the audience. It was a huge departure from his time-honored radio show routine. It required character development — something he doesn't normally do. Each area of comedy is a unique discipline, requiring specific tools, approaches, test appearances, and plenty of rehearsal.

For example, Adam Sandler routinely prepares for talk show appearances by trying out material in his standup routine. He then uses the biographical jokes in his "extemporaneous" talk show interviews. Sandler recognizes that talk show conversation is a unique comedy medium, requiring a different approach.

So, don't be fooled. Improv, character, and sketch comedy require special preparation, just like any other comedy medium.

Receiving Notes

When you first start receiving instructor feedback on your improv or sketch, it's painful. After all, it feels like you offer raw creativity, and the instructor capriciously criticizes you.

To combat this feeling, stop and recognize that the note isn't personal, and it's likely to be a standardized, time-honored, interdisciplinary comedy guideline that will help you for years to come. The more you hear standard criticisms, the less painful they become.

Usually, your first instinct is to justify why the rule doesn't apply to you: "You don't understand! This is different! This is funny because ..." Stop. Take the note. Change your approach immediately. Process the note and bandage your ego later.

Evaluation Criteria

Before you begin your class, you'll naturally wonder what type of performer the company is looking for. Throughout my first improv class, I feared that I would fail. I spent hours nervously pondering my instructor's evaluation criteria. As it turns out, there are no standardized grading criteria. As a coping mechanism, I developed my own criteria for assessing talent. (Some terminology may be new to you. It's explained later in the text.)

- *Presence* — Do you have a unique and dynamic stage presence? Do you have strong interpersonal managerial skills?
- *Rolodexing* — Do you have a cache of specific, unique, interesting information?
- *Foundation* — Can you add information to an improvised scene, including who, what, where, and a theme?
- *Character* — Do you have a physical range, vocal range, and imitative skill?
- *Irony* — Can you convey behavioral and social ironies drawn from your own personal observations?
- *Writing* — Do you have the ability to construct written scenes and monologues using efficient, honed dialogue, with setups and payoffs?

As soon as you establish your own evaluation criteria, you can solidify your own performance goals. Develop your own criteria to help you objectively judge other performers and learn from them.

Performance Reviews

Most schools have mid-class reviews, which attempt to open a dialogue between the instructor and the student, much like a professional performance appraisal.

In The Second City conservatory program, students receive verbal feedback half way through each class. Also, once you're in The Second City Conservatory, you're in. There's little threat of having to retake a class or being asked to discontinue the program. Students stay with the same classmates throughout the entire series of classes, which creates a strong ensemble.

At some schools, students receive written feedback on their strengths and weaknesses. The mid-class review is a harbinger for whether you will pass the class and move to the next level, retake the class, or be asked to study elsewhere. The feedback gives the student a general idea of his progress, and a clue as to whether he'll eventually receive an invitation to join a performance company.

Here's an example of what feedback might look or sound like:

Your ideas and information are good, but the real improv magic comes with "yes anding" your partner. Don't force your preconceived idea. Instead, go with the idea that your partner introduces. If you can do this, it's incredible.

Don't compromise your partner, especially if they are weak. If you do, no one will want to improvise with you.

Play emotions for real. I can tell you're faking it because you drop them so easily. Don't make emotions over-the-top fake, make them over-the-top real. It has to be believable to be funny.

Take classes elsewhere, but be aware of their strengths and weaknesses. Sometimes there's an emphasis on clowning and stealing focus versus "yes anding." For example, one company member is still working on not going for the joke in a scene. Everybody has a learning curve. Good luck in your next class.

It's best to keep communication lines open between you and your instructor throughout the class. The more receptive you are to his feedback, the more likely it is that you'll get honest, direct criticism and advice in return.

The Odds of Making It

At The Second City, the odds of a beginning student making it in to a performance company arc roughly one in one hundred.

In The Groundlings program, on average, roughly one third of the students pass. Another third is asked to repeat the class, and the final third is asked to discontinue. Some students retake classes up to three times, after which they may pass on to the next level or discontinue, at their instructor's discretion. Approximately one in seventy starting students is eventually invited to perform with The Groundlings Sunday Company, and approximately one in one hundred and twenty new students is eventually invited to join the main company. Pretty steep odds.

Tips

The instructor's hardest job is convincing acerbic comedians like you that there really is something to learn beyond trusting your comedic instincts.

Give your fellow players nurturing support. Demonstrate your professionalism.

Some students are blinded by the idea that the top schools are a means for jump-starting their acting careers, and they may not recognize that they're not performance company material. Some students are comedy writers who want to go through the program not to perform, but to experience the writing class.

Whether or not you advance to a performing company, recognize that improv and sketch comedy classes have relevance to screenwriting, television writing, and acting. These principles of comedy apply to dozens of other media and genres — from standup to fiction writing, from the *National Lampoon* to animation, from advertising copy to speechwriting. Recognize the value of improv classes beyond the benefit of acting work.

Where's the "Ensemble" Feeling?

Most comedy performance troupe members have worked together for years. Students, however, are at a disadvantage because they've just met, which accounts for some of the in-class comedy falling flat. Don't beat yourself up about this. Just try to make contact with students whose humor and sensibilities match your own, and maintain contact with those whom you respect and who respect you. Over time, you'll develop "group intuition." You'll join performance groups. Eventually, you'll form long-term working relationships and some nurturing partnerships if you're lucky.

Feedback from Fellow Players

When you work in class, listen to your "approval rating" from your classmates. If fellow players go wild about a character, that's a clue that the character rings true. Likewise, if fellow players give only a lukewarm response, make adjustments and try again. Comedy is always an iterative group effort (even if the "group" is a lone performer and his audience).

Gestation Time

Each class session contains a huge number of new exercises to ponder. Keep a journal of your class sessions. Write down all the exercises and any instructor feedback you receive. You will discover new applications for many of the exercises well after the class is over. Make an effort to *actively* process what you're learning.

Improv as a Profession

Most students recognize that improv is a tool that prepares them for acting and writing. Yes, there is a tiny market for professional improvisers, but even those lucky few are actors and writers. Face it: Improv is an ancillary discipline feeding the soul of comedy in other media.

Be a Jack-of-All-Trades

Few students are jacks-of-all-trades. Some great improv comedians don't do a lot of character work, even though they are incredibly clever, witty performers. Likewise, some expert character actors don't write a lot of sketches. Improv, character creation, and writing feed each other, yet very few players receive letters in all three disciplines. So, challenge yourself by strengthening your weakest area.

Fuzzy Syllabus

The outline of your class isn't set in stone. Instructors seldom review the class objectives at the beginning and end of each session. Sometimes instructors change their syllabi based on time constraints, their own strengths, and your demonstrated skill. So, it's up to you to keep your own outline. Study at as many improv schools as you can to make sure you've learned a variety of techniques and methods.

> *It's strange to me that there's no physical*
> *or vocal warm-up at the start of class. Are these*
> *people actors? Comedians? Writers?*
> *— Author's Journal, May 1, 1999*

Warm-Up

If you haven't studied acting, you may not know the benefits of vocal training. Your voice has to be flexible enough to support a wide range of characters and robust enough to fill the theater. Some students have voices that don't carry onstage and have a surprisingly limited character range — both physically and vocally. Comedy classes don't have time to delve into physical and vocal technique. You'll have to do this outside of class.

> *Tip*
>
> *Improv is confidence-based. The more you improvise, the more confident and relaxed you'll be.*

Perform a physical warm-up before arriving at class. Make a study of *FREEing the Natural Voice* by voice expert Kristen Linklater[1] or other texts on the subject. Take voice classes. Voice exercises increase your relaxation and your awareness of your instrument and its range. The more relaxed, agile, and adaptive your body and voice, the larger your character range will be.

Take stock: After your warm-up, are you more relaxed? Are you in a more creative state with a warm-up than without one? Is your voice more resonant and more audible?

Summary

- *Be normal* in your audition.
- *Instinct and standup comedy experience are not enough.*
- *Prepare to fail forward.* Learn from your mistakes and try again.
- *Keep a journal.*

---

[1] NY: Drama Publishers, 1976.

Section 2
Improv Comedy Basics

*"As soon as I think I've learned these rules … WHAM!
One will hit me from behind when I least expect it.*

*The other day, I thought, 'What is wrong with my dull sketch?'
Then it hit me. I set it in a classroom, with a teacher instructing
the students. Teaching bogs down the scene."*

— Author's Journal, May 20, 2000

Chapter 5

The Enlightenment

Your First Lousy Improv — Help!

The first thing an improv instructor does is test your experience level. He'll ask you to act out a two-person improv scene, giving you nothing but a relationship and location (e.g., dog trainers at a PetSmart). The typical scene lasts three to five minutes, with the instructor stopping the scene when it reaches its peak.

Most of these initial scenes are awful, and they reveal that most of us are novices. (And even if you're an expert, a novice partner can still weigh down your scene.) What these scenes did for me was awaken my sense of need for guidelines — the Comedy Commandments.

Tips

When you start a new class, relax. Resist the tendency to "perform." Instead, listen to your partner and respond naturally.

Look at your partner at the start of the improv. If you're not looking, you're likely not listening.

If you didn't hear your partner, ask them to repeat themselves. Don't risk playing a scene about a "gas leak" when you're partner said "the last geek."

Chapter 6

The Comedy Commandments

As I licked my wounds after my disastrous first improv, the instructor delivered a list of basic comedy rules. (In some schools, the instructor delivers the rules piecemeal throughout the course, not all at once at the beginning.)

The following guidelines apply not only to improv, but to sketch writing and other comedy media, as well. Sure, you can break all the rules. (But learn them first.)

Scenes need "information." Each word, each expression, each movement adds essential data that builds a scene. Add information like who, what, and where. The

> **Tip**
>
> *Keep an ongoing list of rules and techniques as you progress through your classes. Don't wait for someone to hand you a list.*

who is the relationship between characters, their jobs, their attributes, and credentials. The *what* isn't just the action, like watering the lawn, but the emotional level — why are they watering the lawn? The *where* is not geographical, but what comprises the immediate surroundings. What's in the space? Be specific. What objects are available? What attributes does this place have? (See "Falling Anvil #3.")

There are six ways to add information in your scene.

1. **Object work** is stage business — the handling of imaginary objects found in the "where." Give the objects integrity, form and shape. Object work is not gesturing, it's the use of props. In improv, never use real props, and never refer to or remove your own real clothing.

2. **Tempo** is the pace and rhythm of the scene. If your scene stagnates, vary the speed; increase the pace or lurch into slow motion if the scene requires it. By varying or increasing the tempo of your scene, you heighten the intensity and raise the stakes.

3. **Emotions,** or changes in mood, contain information and make the scene important to the characters. Play it big. Feel the emotion, don't talk about it.
4. **Character** is the combination of physical and vocal attributes and a point of view. Character allows the actor to "channel," to become someone else, and to add unusual information that advances the scene.
5. **Stage picture** is the visual image that the players create with their bodies. Change your body position and location during a scene in order to add information about your environment and your point of view. This provides visual appeal. Dig on your hands and knees, collapse on your back, or dance with your partner if the scene requires it.
6. **Dialogue** is information, not just conversation. Never start with "Hello." Start in the middle of the scene. Dialogue should be related to the activity.

Don'ts

Don't negate or deny. *Negating* is the undoing of your partner's information, e.g., "No you didn't!" *Denying* is the refusing of your partner's *offer* (information that advances the scene), e.g., "No, thanks." Always comply in principle with your partner. Sometimes denial is accidental; if it happens, make do.

> *I don't need rules. I'll just get up there and be funny.*
> — *Author's Journal, May 28, 2000*

Don't argue. It's unpleasant. If there's an argument, give in. Don't bargain or haggle. Don't mandate: "I'll give you three seconds until you pick this up." Don't control your partner. You are responsible for your own actions, not your partner's.

Don't instruct or teach. Teaching scenes get bogged down because one player controls the other. It rarely works. Teacher and student characters are fine, but don't teach in the scene.

Don't ask questions. Don't ask what's in the grocery bag; tell them what's in the bag. *Endow* the bag by assigning attributes to it: "I see you bought all proteins, no carbs" or "I see you bought only Nestlé products."

Avoid playing crazy, drunk, blind or under the age of reason. Increase the chances for success in your scene by playing characters who are opinionated, informative, and accountable for their actions. If you must play drunk, play it fully aware. Don't play the cliché trait "old." Avoid playing stupid, deaf, or incapacitated. Avoid playing children, because it limits the scene potential — children are not responsible for their actions. Avoid characters who are irrational, slow to add accurate information, heavily medicated, or who require constant education.

Okay, these rules make sense. How hard can they be to follow?
— Author's Journal, May 29, 2000

Don't plan ahead, just go with the information in front of you. Put your planned idea on the back burner and go with the new reality.

Don't do blue humor. Sex and scatological humor are easy laughs, but they get old quickly. Although some standup comedians make a killing doing it, it's not the smartest material. Shoot for material that is universal in appeal.

Don't be recklessly offensive. Jokes about rape, AIDS, abortion, child molestation, and cancer kill the comedy.

Don't make jokes; play the scene instead.

Don't play strangers. Your characters should know everything about each other. This moves the scene along and reduces exposition. Knowing each other allows you to start in the middle of the conflict and avoid the deadly "Hello, how are you?" scenes.

Don't look at the instructor when you receive a side-coaching during your scene; just incorporate what he says and continue.

Dos

"Yes and" your partner. Listen and respond directly to your partner. Watch your partner; know what he's doing; be aware.

Supply big reactions; don't phone it in. Trust your scene partners. *Give and take.* Put in a little bit and get a response. Don't *drive* (take over) the scene. Discover things onstage. Find something that changes the scene. Allow conflict to arise, but without denying your partner's information.

Work together. Don't be in competition with your fellow players. Don't sacrifice an exercise for a cheap laugh. Make your partner look good. Watch improv and sketch shows to get the hang of it.

Make eye contact. Your partner is half the scene. Look into your partner's eyes and grow the scene together.

What Good Are These "Comedy Commandments"?

These guidelines are mostly for improvisation and comedy writing, but there are benefits to other comedy disciplines, too — from radio to film. For example, if a morning radio comedy show is lagging, it's because the call-in guest says "Hi, how are you?" instead of jumping into a topic. If a scene in an "indie" film is flat, it's probably because the foundation is too abstract — we don't know who, what, and where. If a sitcom scene is slow, it may be that the characters aren't playing to the top of their intelligence or they're arguing. You will come back to these rules again and again, discovering new applications as you create characters and write sketch comedy. Each of these rules will be covered in detail throughout the text.

> *Tip*
>
> Improv is like a muscle, the more you exercise, the stronger and more agile your improv becomes.

Take stock: In my first class, there were so many rules to learn that I was overwhelmed. "How do I keep all these plates spinning at once?" Generally, after a year or so, the rules become second nature.

Summary
- *You won't need rules* until after your first bad improv.
- *Break the rules,* but learn them first.
- *The rules apply to all comedy media.* You'll come back to them again and again.

Chapter 7

Four Falling Anvils of Improv

*"I'm not worried about my first class. I'll just use my usual shtick,
and they'll love me. No problem. I mean, I'm the epicenter
of comedy at parties. My wit is a registered weapon.
Besides, you can't teach someone to be funny.
I'm sure I'll do fine at improv."*
— Author's Journal, November 24, 2000

The bad news didn't hit me until I improvised in class: I had a lot to learn. Sure, I had good comedic instincts, but it wasn't enough. There were guidelines that I had to learn in order to turn my comedic instincts into funny improv, characters, and sketches. I had to learn the hard way, by being beaten into enlightenment by the proverbial unexpected falling anvil. You will too.

Here are the four essential concepts, or falling anvils, that form the groundwork for improv, character, and sketch comedy:

Falling Anvil #1: Collaboration
Falling Anvil #2: Agreement
Falling Anvil #3: Foundation: Who, What, and Where
Falling Anvil #4: Exploring, Heightening, and Finding a Game

It takes years to master these scene skills. Because these four skills are so involved, and so critical, each appears in a separate chapter, along with selected exercises. These skills are so fundamental to comedy that you'll return to them frequently.

Chapter 8

Falling Anvil # 1: Collaboration

Wake up and stop thinking about "performing." The magic of improv comes from the power of two. You and your partner. The sooner you realize that improv is a collaboration, the sooner you'll become aware of the importance of the players next to you.

Group Mind

Two or more players improvising in perfect unison is a blessed event to behold. It's the result of focused work, although it appears accidental. This phenomenon is the result of an ensemble awareness skill called *Group Mind.*

Group Mind exercises appear in every level of improv comedy class, from beginner to expert. Group Mind exercises have hidden benefits that help comedy performers:

- *Break the ice.*
- *Watch and listen to their partner.*
- *Relinquish control.*
- *Get out of their head and into their instincts.*
- *Playfully explore language, movement, and dialogue.*

> *"I don't need exercises to develop a 'group mind'. I just want to know why my improv scenes aren't working."*
> *— Author's Journal, November 25, 2000*

Group Mind exercises are well documented in Spolin's *Improvisation for the Theater.* A select group of preferred exercises appears in the appendix on page 163. Here's a sample Group Mind exercise:

> **Machines**
>
> Five to six players. In this classic theater game, Player One starts alone onstage, making a repeating rhythmic motion with sound, representing a part of a machine, e.g., a treasury printing press. The next player joins in as an adjacent part, adding a different repeating motion with sound, physically connected with Player One in some way. When all players have joined, the instructor suggests an emotion, and the machine takes on the new emotion, changing the rhythm, tempo, and attitude.

I didn't realize at first, but this silly "machines" exercise covers so many improv objectives: listening, agreement, group awareness, give and take, awareness of the stage picture, emotional agreement, scene tempo. (It even has a built-in comedic structure of "random emotions" used frequently in sketch comedy and even film.) Avoid dismissing any exercise as "whimsical introductory junk."

Rolodexing

Rolodexing is the mental skill of creating and retrieving unique information on a topic. Players "rolodex" information before and during an improv in order to retrieve their funniest thoughts on a given topic. For example, if the improv topic is the "stock market," the expressions "Dot Bomb," "NASDAQ," and "Footsie 500 Index" are more specific and entertaining than just the words "dividends" and "shares." When you rolodex, you can:

- *Support the scene's premise with specific, intelligent, topical ideas.*
- *Build an entertaining character point of view.*
- *Justify seemingly disparate information in the scene.*

At first, the following Group Mind and Rolodexing exercises may seem whimsical and repetitive, but as you get experience performing, you'll know that these skills are paramount for adding smart information to improvised scenes. Descriptions for all exercises appear in the appendix on page 163. Here is a sample Rolodexing exercise.

···

Topic Firing Line (a.k.a. *Firing Squad* or *Ru Ru Ru*)
Group. In this exercise developed by George McGrath of The Groundlings, all players line up for a rapid-fire competition. The instructor calls out a category, like "soap operas," and each player steps forward in turn with commitment and boldly announces the made-up name of a soap opera, e.g., "Brunch and Divorce" or "Lipstick on the World's Collar." The instructor eliminates players who repeat, hesitate, lack commitment, or break character. Some instructors change the topic midstream. As a variation, the instructor calls out an absurdly complicated or technical question and the players must answer briefly, resolutely, and confidently. The focus of this exercise is rolodexing, concentration, and commitment to the ridiculous.

···

Helpful Hints

Warm-up Exercises

Classic group warm-up exercises, detailed in the appendix on page 162, will warm up your voice and body and exercise your ability to listen. You will begin to develop a group mind, rolodex, and start to create stories together. Here is a sample exercise from this category:

···

Tug of War — Imaginary Rope
Group. All players divide into two teams. Upon the instructor's command, the teams play tug of war with an imaginary rope. As the teams pull, the rope must retain its form. This is harder than it sounds. Teams must agree to give and take, carefully observing their fellow players in order to maintain the integrity of the mimed rope. Eventually, players realize that in order to make a scene work, they must give up control and act as part of a whole.

···

This exercise has meaning beyond simple object work. In two-person improvs you'll likely find yourself in a "tug of war" with a headstrong improviser. Give and take, listen to your partner, agree with him, follow his lead, mirror him, and hope he does the same for you.

Bailing

Never bail (give up) in an improv that is floundering. Even the most experienced improvisers get stuck in faulty improvs — one player hogs the stage, the scene is wandering aimlessly, or the subject matter is unappealing. There is a way to breathe new life into it.

Whenever something is going wrong in an improv, use it. Call the reality of the scene. "Gee, there's a lot going on here — your family is complicated like a soap opera." Or, "Say, you sure are verbose for a farmer!" Or, "I thought this game show was about Hollywood trivia, but it's really about insulting the players!" Whatever is going through your mind about a messy scene is probably pretty close to what others are thinking, too. Identify how you're really feeling about the problem and use it.

Improvised Scenes in Class Are Longer

At this point, you'll start to recognize that improvised scenes that you perform in class last about seven minutes, but improvised scenes performed for an audience last only about three to five minutes. Instructors extend class improvs for two reasons. First, novice players take longer to set up the scene and find a through-line. Second, the instructor wants to challenge students to see if they can pick a scene up if it falls down. Can you continue an improv, even though it has lulled? Can you give an improv new life with a second through-line, even though the first one has already run its course? So, even though class improvs aren't necessarily performance-ready, you're exercising muscles that you'll use in performance.

31

Take stock: It's easy to dismiss these exercises as frivolous until you see the positive results. Now that you are warmed up and have a group mind, you can begin to establish two-person stories. To do so successfully, you must get into the mindset of agreement.

Summary

- *Warm up* before your class.
- *Focus on your partner.*
- *Create a group mind* — it builds intuition.
- *Rolodex* unique information before and during your improv.
- *Never bail* from an improv. Stick with it.

Chapter 9

Falling Anvil #2: Agreement

When you start to improvise simple stories, agreement with your scene partner is critical.

"Every word your partner says is a gift." When you first hear this slogan, you dismiss it as being remedial theater advice for newbies. However, it's more important than that. It means what it says. Table your own preconceived idea, and listen to your partner, especially if they're a weak improviser. Support your partner's idea instead. Whatever they say, goes — because without your compliance, you won't have a scene at all. If you're able to rolodex twenty-three ideas right before the scene starts, you'll surely make a terrific new choice based on the awful idea your partner just gave you. Agree to follow each other. Together.

Just Say "Yes"

> *"If everyone says 'yes' in the scene, doesn't that sap the conflict? Doesn't that deflate the humor in the scene?"*
> — Author's Journal, November 25, 2000

When I was a new student of improv, I incorrectly assumed that an improv required conflict and plot, just like plays and sitcoms. However, conflict is as easy to generate as the word "no."

Player One: *Let's get married.*
Player Two: *No.*

Instant conflict. And although it may generate a laugh, it's a dead end to the improv. Short-term gain, long-term loss.

"Yes," on the other hand, opens the world of possibility and the world of endless irony.

Player One: *Let's get married.*
Player Two: *Yes! No better place than here at the Winter Olympics.*
Player One: *I hope we can find a priest who can luge.*
Player Two: (Waxing his sled) *Yeah, and doesn't mind laying on top of us during the ceremony on the way down the course.*
Player One: *And ... And ... And ...*

Saying "Yes" — even a reluctant "Yes" — gives the scene momentum. However, saying "No" gets a small laugh followed by a very long silence as the scene dies.

For those neophytes who are still clinging to "No" to generate a laugh, here's a secret: "Yes" gives you much more to work with — it creates new obstacles that you hurdle together, brings on pain you both endure, and presents problems you must continuously solve with your partner. "No" forces you to continually find something else to do, which is tiresome for both you and the audience.

Practice re-wording your funny negative statements into funny positive ones that move the scene forward:

Funny denials that shut down an improv.	*Funny "yes ands ..." that advance the scene.*
No, I won't give you the last parachute. I have a wife and 3.5 kids at home!	Okay, take the last parachute. Tell my 3.5 kids I didn't make it. In fact, here's a list of things I want you to tell them.
No, I won't dance with you. You're a man. I'm a man.	I'll slow dance *one song only!* This class reunion is different than I expected.
Stealing this Toyota Camry is immoral. I can't.	I know stealing this Toyota Camry is immoral, but I'll do it anyway because I've got to get to my wedding. I need cash to pay the priest ... check the glove compartment.

Most witty people, even successful comedians, make the mistake of responding "No" when they begin improvising. They're used to getting laughs with sitcom dialogue, like this excerpt from *The Golden Girls*:

> **Rose:** *Want some breakfast?*
> **Sophia:** *Not if you're making it!*

In sitcoms arguing, negation, and denial are usually callbacks to previously established information. Denying doesn't work in improv — it's a three-minute medium where you start from scratch each time the lights come up. So, abandon your impulse to say "No" for a short-term laugh, and instead, say "Yes" and build a scene about ghastly microwaveable breakfast blintzes.

The following exercise is the basis for all of improv and appears at every major improv school. It emphasizes the primary requirement of comedy: Scene partners must agree and focus on the same thing in order to spontaneously create a random scene with a single point of focus, find a through-line in that scene, and explore it. You must give and take and be willing to turn on a dime.

Tips

If you get stuck in an argument, give in and justify why.

Do agreement and mirroring exercises backstage before a performance. When you agree, you build unique scenes with completely original premises.

Most improv newbies create frantic scenes with too much going on because they don't focus on their partner's information, and then "Yes and" it.

Favor the downstage center area during your improv. (The more frightened and tense you are, the farther upstage you'll go.)

"Yes, and" (a.k.a. *Story/Story)*
This exercise is commonly used at all schools. Two players sit facing each other. Player One starts a story with a single, short sentence in past tense. Player Two confirms what his partner says and adds to it, starting with the words "Yes, and you ... " Player One continues with "Yes, and I ... " and so on. Keep the sentences short and action-oriented.

> **Player One:** I made a ghost costume for Halloween.
> **Player Two:** Yes, and you cut the eye holes too small.
> **Player One:** Yes, and I bumped into things.
> **Player Two:** Yes, and you got hit by a car.
> **Player One:** Yes, and I landed on the sidewalk.
> **Player Two:** Yes, and you called an ambulance.
> **Player One:** Yes, and I had to convince the medics I was not a blind ghost.

"I don't need 'Yes and.' I need a decent partner
who will accept my great idea and go along
with it without getting in my way."
— Author's Journal, November 29, 2000

During this exercise, focus on what's fun in a scene, and talk about it. If you won $40,000 at blackjack, focus on the win. How did it happen? Who was there to witness it?

Be conscious of dead-ending your partner by terminating their thought. Instead, focus on what your partner introduced and further its detail. Also, introduce a new train of thought only when the current one has run its course. If you introduce a new train of thought, keep it in the same theme or subject.

Avoid diluting the importance of an action. If your partner says, "I went to the store, and it was closed," and you say, "Yes, and you went to another store, and it was closed, too," you haven't added new information. Instead, *raise the stakes*. Heighten the importance for every statement. "Yes, and I was so angry I stayed overnight in the parking lot until they opened!" Also, further the funny or interesting part of the previous statement. If the audience laughs, "click" on that idea, and advance it.

"Yes and" is the basis for all improv because it forces you to *instantly, excessively* agree with your partner's information.

Don't Argue

Sketches by Abbott and Costello ("Who's on First"), Fibber McGee and Molly, and Burns and Allen are full of great comedic arguments. However, these are scripted arguments, with a hidden understructure of agreement that keeps the scene moving forward. Improv is unscripted and, as a result, more fragile.

Benefits to Agreement

Agreement is the cure for any ailing improv. Agreement helps you do the following:

- *Avoid annoying arguments* that are hard on the ears
- *Establish who, what, and where* more easily when the information is freely flowing without obstruction
- *Create whimsical characters* more easily when players mirror each other
- *Explore the absurd situation* and allow the unique information to expand and build
- *Heighten the scene* by advancing the absurd elements in the scene instead of shutting them down with disagreement

Agree, at a Price

In normal circumstances, your character would probably say "No" to certain offers, but the improv rule is to say "Yes." Instead of saying "No," agree to the offer reluctantly and then add why your agreeing will make it difficult for you. In other words, identify the character's sacrifice in saying "Yes."

> *Player One:* Okay. Even though I should buy a pacemaker, I'll buy these Blaupunkt stereo speakers, instead. The sound of that woofer is incredible!

Positive Start

A *positive start* is an improv technique that uses agreement to give your scene a quick, unique setup with room to grow. To give your scene a positive start, agree with each other; mirror your

---

Tips

Avoid seeking conflict in improv. Instead, build a ridiculous world together, where the characters work against their predicament.

Don't fix problems. Make them worse. Even if a character's objective is to try to make it better, he tries to no avail, and the problem worsens.

"Wherever you go, you take your sh** with you." In other words, avoid going somewhere else *in your improv — once you get there, you still have to set up the scene. (You won't find a better scene to play over* there, *so, get to it* here.*)*

---

partner's emotion, character, and activity; and avoid being downbeat. A positive start helps you:
- *Invite unique, offbeat information into the scene*
- *Avoid a tedious argument*
- *Establish the "normal world,"* ripe for havoc

Avoid Starting with Negative Statements
Starting with a whiney, negative statement will dampen the audience's mood.

> *Player One: Fishing sucks.*

The action stops before it even starts. If your character hates the activity, he wouldn't be here. Instead, find some joy in why you're here and identify your obstacle.

> *Player One: This lake is stocked with massive fish. Yesterday I caught a thirteen-pound bluegill. It fought me for two hours. Now I'm afraid to put my line in the water!*

Even when your partner starts negatively, agree.

> *Player One: You're so stupid for buying this oil rig.*
> *Player Two: I am so stupid for buying this oil rig! The man who sold it to me convinced me it would be a Shangri-La, and now I'm stuck working here! I'm so stupid!*

And another:

> *Player One: Collecting matchbooks is dangerous because of the fire risk.*
> *Player Two: It's so dangerous! We're the only couple on the block to collect historic items that are combustible. Like these 1950s Amoco gas cans. See, this one's full.*

As soon as there is agreement on the premise, you avoid an argument and you create an instant through-line — this ridiculous couple loves what they collect, but it could kill them at any moment.

Cop an Attitude

Without an opinion in the first line, there's no point of view, no irony, no objective, and no inherent premise. Don't settle for "There are seven years' worth of leaves to rake here." Instead, cry out "There are seven years' worth of leaves to rake here — my teenage life is ruined!" The second statement contains an emotional point of view, and thus solidifies the premise quickly.

Avoid Denying and Negating

Denying is the refusing, ignoring, or diluting of a partner's offer.

> **Player One:** *Have a mint for fresh breath.*
>
> **Player Two:** *No thanks, I just had my teeth cleaned at Sears Dental.*

Tips

Improvs that start with whining or an angry argument are hard on the ears. Instead, give your scene a positive start.

When your character says "I'm bored. Let's get out of here," the audience is thinking the same thing.

The first line out should contain an opinion or attitude.

If a player negates what you said, then agree with both pieces of information, e.g., first you call your partner "Ethel" and later someone calls her "Barbara," then call her "Ethel-Barbara."

Now what? Player Two denied the offer of a scene about mints. Both players must now discover something else to play, bringing the scene to a screeching halt. Say yes, instead. Discover something amazing about the flavor. Or establish that you both work at the Stinking Rose, a garlic restaurant, despite it ruining your breath and your social life.

Also, avoid *negating*, which is the outright undoing of your partner's information.

> **Player One:** *Have a mint for fresh breath.*
> **Player Two:** *That's not a mint! That's Crystal Draino!*

Although a negation gets a short-term laugh, it undermines the fragile reality established by the players. Eventually, players and audience can't tell what's real, what's not, or why.

So, the beginning of improv scenes are incredibly fragile, needing lots of confirmation and agreement.

An Offer You Just Can't Deny

Denial sometimes creeps into scenes, even with *experienced* players:

> **Player One:** *That's because you're a kleptomaniac.*
> **Player Two:** *I'm in remission!*

Player Two denied the offer, dulling the impact of the label "kleptomaniac." In improv, don't be "latent," and don't delay the action. In a three-minute medium, there's no time for secrets — reveal them right away. So, accept your partner's offer at face value. If your partner labels your character a "klepto," be a raging, unstoppable klepto whose attic is stuffed full of *objects d'art*. Get right to the fun parts — exposing his problem, mocking his failing recovery efforts, or skewering him for hoarding worthless chotchke.

Even if your partner denies you, incorporate his denial into the scene.

> **Player One:** *That's because you're a kleptomaniac.*
> **Player Two:** *I'm in remission!*
> **Player One:** *Sorry, I should have said "kleptomaniac in remission." Let's return these "found objects" to their "owners."*
> **Player Two:** *Thanks for understanding I'm "ownership disoriented."*

So, Player Two *used* the denial and made it productive — the scene is now about walking on eggshells with a recovering klepto.

If you're an advanced student, you'll learn to accept your partner's offer using *constructive non-cooperation* (advancing the scene while maintaining the obstacle). For example, if you're labeled a confrontational cop, become confrontational, but make an extra effort to advance the action in the

Tips

Even if your partner denies you, incorporate his denial into the scene.

Avoid "unmasking" yourself in improv. Avoid "I'm really a CIA operative and you fell for my trap!" or "I was just testing you." If you negate the established information, you leave the scene back at square one — who, what, and where.

40

scene, not shut it down with outright argument. Or, if you're labeled a nurse and the patient asks you to release his restraints, you may productively say "No," and tease him sexually, building a scene about a mental hospital full of teasing vixen nurses. (You accepted your partner's offer to build a scene about the restraints.) As you gain experience, you'll sense the difference between denying that shuts down a scene and constructive non-cooperation, which advances it.

Nothing Pre-Planned

Nothing in improv is pre-planned, not even one second before (even if the scene has a pre-established who, what, and where). Start by observing your partner, the silent body language, and the emotion of your characters. Each element builds on the next. Not until these elements are revealed can you know what the scene is about. The premise is developed in the moment. It's unveiled gradually in each second. It changes second by second as the information unveils. Don't feel pressured to lay on information from nowhere. Use the clues in front of you.

Give yourself over to not knowing. Throw away your preconceived ideas at the beginning, and give in to the new instant mutual discovery. Take your time to discover the scene together. Leap and the net will appear.

If your partner is rowing a boat and you say, "This airplane has first rate food!" it won't correspond to what she's doing. Everyone in the audience knows you offered a pre-planned idea.

To avoid planning ahead in improv, do the New Choice exercise below. New Choice is an old standard in use at all schools.

New Choice

The New Choice exercise encourages you to go with an idea that just popped into your head, based on the information your partner gave you *just now*. Two players develop a scene with a given what or where, as usual. Then the instructor calls out "New choice!" forcing the player who is talking to finish his sentence with a new random piece of information. Here's an example:

41

Player One: Charlie, give me your breakfast order.
Player Two: This morning, I want pancakes.
Director: New choice!
Player Two: This morning, I want a striptease.
Director: New choice!
Player Two: This morning, I want a science experiment ... because I like to see explosions before I go to my boring accounting job.
Player One: One explosion special coming up.

So, each time the instructor calls out "New choice!" the player produces random endings for his sentence. Once the player offers a new choice that is acceptable, the instructor stops calling "new choice." Now, the player must justify the most recent information. (*Justifying* is making logical sense of an absurdity by adding supporting information.) The scene continues based on the new information until the instructor calls out "New Choice" again.

All improv should feel this way. Everything that happens in at the start of a scene should be a logical surprise that you justify, support, and elaborate on.

Take stock: At this point you have practiced creating stories with the "Yes and" exercise. You're aware of the benefits of agreement, giving a positive start to your scene, and making new choices in the moment based on your partner's idea. Next, let's build a scene's foundation.

Summary
- *Accept your partner's offer.* Agree.
- *Use a positive start.* Avoid arguing, negating, and denying.
- *Justify* the anomalies in the scene. Make sense of them.
- *Avoid planning ahead.* Give yourself over to not knowing.

Chapter 10

Falling Anvil #3: Foundation (Who, What, and Where)

The third falling anvil addresses the basic components of drama, the *foundation* — who the characters are, where they are, and what they're doing. This expository information is vital to building a relatable scene. Without identifying who, what, and where, your scene will resemble bad performance art.

Object Work

Start with the simplest of the three — the "what." Begin with a solo exercise called Everyday Task.

Everyday Task (Object Work Exercise)
In this standard exercise based on one originated by Uta Hagen, you prepare a silent solo scene to practice object work — the handling of imaginary props. The actor uses his imaginary props downstage center, along the invisible *fourth wall.*

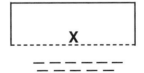

Figure 2

The *fourth wall* is the line separating actor and audience, along the downstage edge of the playing space (see figure 2). (Most improv comedy stages are "proscenium arch" style.) Avoid doing object work upstage left or right, as you'll probably turn your back and cut yourself off from the audience. Do object work *down center*, facing

---

the audience, where everyone can see. Downstage center is the focal point for object work.

The Everyday Task scene is the re-created essence of a daily routine, like entering the kitchen and pouring a morning glass of milk. The specificity with which you enter and handle your imaginary props reveals information about your character, your history, environment, point of view, and even emotions. In rehearsal, experienced actors include the interesting aspects of the daily routine and edit out the dull parts. The editing process is the key to building heightened comic premises.

Tips

Always use the fourth wall for object work, condensing all the needed objects along the downstage area, where players and audience can see. Even if someone creates a car, then magically align the car along the fourth wall.

Object work can save a stagnant scene. Discovering objects in the environment can give your scene a point of focus.

Don't bring on real props or costumes in improv. Real props are finite and limit the potential of a scene. (A real cup is worthless without a table to set it on, and a napkin, etc.)

While you watch the others perform the Everyday Task exercise, think about what you might say to that character if you were in the scene with them. For example, if a player is eating, you may imagine yourself saying, "Rich, honey, let your wife make you her 'pantry special' late night snack — it will help you gain weight for your wrestling match tomorrow." This sentence neatly defines who, what, and where.

Now that you have explored object work as a way to establish your character and environment without words, let's practice the art of defining *who, what,* and *where* using dialogue.

Setting Up the Foundation

The *foundation* of a scene is *who* you are, *what* you're doing, and *where* you're doing it. On screen, some of these expository elements are relayed visually. On an empty stage, however, you must label the foundation using expository dialogue. It takes practice. Everyday conversation doesn't normally contain high-powered back-story. Nevertheless, in improv, it's necessary. Short scenes require quick, efficient setups.

Carefully look at the following two-line exchange. We know an incredible amount about this scene in just two improvised lines.

> *Player One: Marcy, it's exciting to have a sister packing her bags to join a cult!*
> *Player Two: I'm joining the God Rangers tonight, Precious. I'm escaping through our bedroom window.*

Who: Marcy and Precious (sisters)
Where: Their bedroom with a window
What: One is packing her bags and running away to a cult, the God Rangers
Other assumed information: They're likely under 18. Marcy is radical; Precious follows the rules and is probably the favored child. Marcy is probably escaping through a second-floor window because she wants to avoid her parents. Marcy has clothes and a suitcase. Based on the name, the God Rangers may be a religious cult with environmental ties.

Tips

New improvisers clutch the bowl of cookie dough as if their life depended on it. Object work is only one component of a scene and should be used to subtly support the scene's premise.

The "what" is more than just object work. It's finding the through-line in the scene. For example, the "what" isn't just your fixing a wheel on your red wagon; it's realizing that every toy your parents gave you in your childhood was broken.

"First line out" means that the first spoken line usually sets up the scene's action. The first line out usually determines who the characters are, what their attitudes are, and what the focus of the scene is.

Ask Fors

Before an improv starts, the instructor may request a scene suggestion from classmates (or an audience), like who, what, where, or other information. This is called an *ask for*. The more ask fors you have before the improv starts, the less work you'll have to do to establish this information from scratch.

In basic classes, you'll lay out the who, what, and where right away, just for practice. However, in more advanced classes, it's critical that you to establish this information organically, as the clues to the scene *gradually* unfold.

If you have ever seen bad improv, it's likely bad because the players are floating in limbo — they haven't identified who they are, where they are, or what they're doing. The clearer these elements, the more the audience can relate. The following exercise (in use at The Second City, The Groundlings, and many other schools) forces you to verbalize the foundation.

ginning improv
es, the instructor
provides the who,
t, or where to help
up the scene. In
anced classes, players
required to do it
mselves.

an improv bombs, it's
:ely the lack of
undation: who, what,
nd where. If you don't
dd these seemingly
nnocuous tidbits, your
mprov wanders
aimlessly.

Eventually, adding the
foundation becomes
second nature.
Sometimes expert players
create such a focused
premise that they don't
need to label the whole
foundation.

Add Info Lineup (a.k.a. *Short Scenes or Two Lines*)
In this exercise created by Phyllis Katz and Cathy Shambley of The Groundlings, players assemble into two lines. The first players from each line pair up. Player One starts object work and Player Two observes and joins in. In conversation, Player One identifies the other player by name or occupation (who) and then identifies what they are doing (what). Player Two responds by identifying Player One by name (who) and where their specific location is (where):

Player One: Who. What.
Player Two: Who. Where.

Once the information is out, the scene is finished. The next pair of players in line begin a new scene. In other words, each player adds information about who they are, what they're doing, and where they're doing it, and they're done. Sure, the information is a little forced, but the focus is on practicing the who/what/where platform.

This exercise also forces the players to be in the moment, adding information based on what they're doing right now, not on a preconceived idea from three seconds earlier.

Player One: *Prince Evan! You're preparing frozen dinners for your guests!*
Player Two: *I'm cost-cutting, Jeeves, because we British royals are suddenly out of favor. By the way, your salary is cut in half, and you'll be sleeping here in the castle kitchen with me.*

The Add Info Lineup exercise is difficult at first because it combines so many basic skills of improv all at once:

- *Listen* and watch your partner for clues.
- *Make new choices* in the moment. "Yes and."
- *Provide logical information*, not from "outer space."
- *Build the foundation* succinctly: who, what, and where
- *Make exposition less clunky.* Not, "Cassia, I'm your husband here in our kitchen making dinner as a way to make up for our fight." But rather, "Good husbands like me make up after a fight by doing KP duty, Cassia."
- *Give a reason for your activity.* Reveal the high-stakes emotional reason why you are doing this activity, here and now. Not just "I'm filling the gas tank." But rather, "Sorry, I forgot to fill the limousine with gas before your wedding, Mr. Lowry. Please be an understanding groom."

47

Tips

Avoid the cliched "dating" scenario. Instead, open your mind to the million relationships between partners, e.g., landlord and tenant, common law husband and wife, plastic surgeon and patient. The comedy comes from the specificity of the relationship.

Never say "I don't know" or "I'm not sure." It's un-dramatic. Immediately adopt a specific attitude and intention.

Don't ask questions. Instead, answer your own questions with specific information. Avoid "What are you reading?" Rather, state that "studying for three days without sleep is not going to help you pass the Bar exam." Specifics build a scene quickly.

Practice making the line you say do four things at once: set up the foundation, "yes and" the other player, reveal your point of view, and display an emotion. In the heat of performance, you may only manage to do one of these things.

Exercises — Practice Adding the Foundation

Practice adding foundational elements (who, what, where, object work, tempo changes, emotion, and stage picture) using the exercises in the appendix on page 167.

Practice Building the Foundation Alone

At the risk of being schizophrenic, play two roles when you're outside of class and don't have a partner. That is, try writing a series of opening first lines of dialogue containing a "who" and "what." Later, when you've forgotten what you've written, go back to the same list and respond spontaneously with a second line of dialogue for each first line, including a who and a where.

Player One: Take this bribe, Father. I want you to break the rules and marry me to a Jewish girl.
Player Two: ?

Player One: Mr. Rapier, I sold you my house, and you painted it a different color. My childhood memories are ruined!
Player Two: ?

Player One: This Mazda Miata is perfect for a sexy single professional like you, looking for a little excitement.
Player Two: ?

Helpful Hints

Keep the following in mind when building the foundation.

Avoid "Laying On" Information

The Add Info Lineup exercise encourages you to expedite the who, what, and where *just for practice*. However, as a rule, don't unilaterally "lay on" unprecedented information at the start of an improv.

> **Player One:** *It's time to repaint this foyer! After all, it's been three months since we decorated, and we're the Hampton's premiere couple.*

Whoa! Too much information from one player! Too much information from outer space! Instead, let the information *naturally* arise from the clues in front of you: the object work, the stage picture, the emotions, the character, and the dialogue. Add a piece of information and shut up. Let your partner respond. "Yes and" your partner. Give and take. Build the scene gradually and economically. Make a new choice, naturally arising out of something your partner says. Adapt. Create a weird world together. Discover your world's incongruities together, piece by piece.

Know Everything Already

Play to the top of your character's intelligence in order to make your scene efficient and eventful. Your character must know everything already: who they're talking with, their problems, and their specific point of view. Start in the middle of the scene.

> ## *Tip*
> Don't control the scene. Give and take. Two heads are better than one. (If the scene bombs, you're only half to blame.)

When you uncover a new truth, already have an instant, emotional opinion about it, confirm the information, justify it, and heighten the problem.

Not knowing, asking questions:

> **Player One:** *I sold your clothes so I could buy this Elvis on velvet painting.*
> **Player Two:** *What? How could you sell my clothes? Dammit! Why did you do that?*

Already knowing, advancing the scene:

Player One: I sold your clothes so I could buy this Elvis on velvet painting.

Player Two: Great! We're one step closer to financing a shrine to Elvis, whatever the cost! Tomorrow I'm selling my kidney!

Avoid being confused, incredulous, or uninformed, which all slow down the scene. There's no time for instruction, evading, or guessing — these things delay the action. Get right to the fun part.

For example, if Player One is secretly drinking on the job, Player Two must expose her problem right away. Player One must admit her drinking problem immediately. (No time for evasion — reveal the truth, pronto.) Now comes the fun part. Maybe you find all her expensive, imported scotch; or you find her personal distillery hidden in the office. By the time you find the gist of the scene, explore it, and heighten it, the scene is over, confirming that there was no time for a secret, after all.

Become Emotional

Becoming emotional raises the stakes of a scene, because your character is fully invested in the problem. Emotions create instant character objectives that advance the scene.

As an exercise outside of class, review the four basic emotions often called for in a scene: happiness, sadness, anger, and fear. Write a list of other derivative emotional states, e.g., forlorn, humiliated, grieving, effervescent, giddy. Emotions and character attributes heighten a scene by rooting you in a specific, active point of view.

Use the Stage Picture

The *stage picture* is the visual image that the players create with their bodies. During scenes, use your body to add information about your environment, your point of view, and to provide visual appeal. Sometimes an entire improvised scene can be done without words, with the characters creating a relationship, activity, and environment with just their bodies.

Change the Tempo

The basic comedy rule "faster, louder, funnier" has its place. A lively tempo keeps the scene's information flowing — ahead of the audience's expectations. A gradual increase in tempo subliminally informs the audience about the understructure of the scene (they sense that the scene is heightening to absurd proportions, ready for the blackout). An unchanging tempo, however, can sap your scene's momentum. (Avoid a pace that *starts* frantic and *stays* frantic throughout — you'll have nowhere to go.) Allow the heightening action of the scene to influence your pace.

Add Character/Point of View

Now that you have practiced laying the foundation with who, what, and where, using object work, tempo changes, emotion, and the stage picture to advance the scene, give your character a specific point of view. Your charater's attitude and demeanor will reveal specific intentions and advance the scene.

Object Work Creates a Character

In this exercise based on a Spolin classic, the entire group walks around in a random pattern. While players are moving, the instructor assigns a job credential for everyone, like "Congressman." Keep moving, use the emotion, find object work — objects in this person's environment — and begin speaking as the character. Remember, object work isn't just movement for movement's sake, and it's not gesturing. It's a specific action that focuses on the detail of this character's life. For example, if your character is a congressman, you might start first by picking up a quill pen (object work), which triggers a random emotion, like "resentful." Your dialogue might be something like:

Player One: I always have to sign these damn declarations with my signature underneath Samuel Adams'. I'm always in his shadow. I might just spill some ink accidentally here … "

The instructor lets the characters speak briefly (simultaneously). Next, the instructor repeats the exercise with a different character, pointing to each player to give a brief solo speech. The specificity of job (who) and object work (what) in an environment (where) establishes a character instantly.

Tips

Avoid talking about the emotion. "I am so angry." Instead, be the emotion and tell us why.

In any improv, you can prove to your fellow players that you're "Yes, anding" what they say by reiterating some of their words in your line.

Avoid making two-person scenes only about the object work; the scene is about the relationship and why they're here right now. Object work is only part of the "what."

Echo Your Partner's Line

Two-person scene, with a given "where." The players start a scene as usual, establishing the foundation, but they're required to repeat a word or phrase from the other character's dialogue in order to prove a direct "Yes and." This forces players to agree on a single point of focus.

You can "Yes and" information and still move the scene forward. Make sure to progress the scene by exploring emotion and object work. Don't get too bogged down in minutiae.

Player One: Mr. Klein, as your designer, I can assure you that these low rise jeans will take the fashion world by storm!

Player Two: We'll create a storm of controversy over low rise jeans. Controversy means sales! In fact, let's make 'em real low! Lower! Lower!

Take stock: Now that you have practiced establishing scenes with who, what, and where, with the aid of agreement, object work, tempo changes, emotion, character, and stage picture, begin to explore the premise of the scene.

Summary

- *Use object work* to help establish the character and environment.
- *Set up the foundation.* Tell us who, what, and where, using dialogue.
- *Avoid laying on information.* Use the clues in front of you, instead.
- *Advance the scene.* Add emotion, object work, change the stage picture, change the tempo, and add a character's point of view.

Chapter 11

Falling Anvil #4: Exploring, Heightening, and Finding a Game

After I became comfortable agreeing and building the foundation, my scenes would somehow stagnate. My scenes were chock full of great information, emotion, object work, and a changing stage picture, but without a strong through-line. The cure for this is to explore, heighten, and find a game. Here's how.

Exploring

Once you have laid out the foundation (who, what, and where), begin to explore. *Exploring* is the process of making discoveries in your environment, your activity, your emotion, your character, and your relationship. As you explore, pay attention to the information you discover. For example, you may discover that you are making cookies. Then, you may discover that your partner is holding a boat oar. And, you may discover you are happily married.

Don't ignore these incongruent pieces of information; they are your clues to finding a tilt.

> *"All my improvs are a frantic mish-mash of unrelated incidents: an alien abduction, a tsunami, and a visit by Charles Nelson Reilly, all in the same scene. Help!"*
> — Author's Journal, December 2, 2000

Finding the Tilt

The *tilt* is anything in your scene that is abnormal, an aberration from the status quo, or a disruption in the characters' everyday routine.

In this example, you are making cookies and your husband is holding a boat oar. Why? Because you're making the world's largest batch of chocolate chip cookies — stirred with a boat oar.

You discover this tilt in the scene by accident. The tilt appears in the moment, based on the difference in your object work. The tilt can present itself based on any incongruous information — the difference between your voices or accents, something unusual in your environment, or anything that strikes you as being out of the ordinary.

So, you must justify *why* this absurdity is so. For example, you can establish that these parents placate their spoiled children with large quantities of baked goods.

Expanding on the Tilt

Now, *extend*, or expand the tilt into a full blown game. The *game* is a theme or pattern in the character's lives that repeats and escalates for comic effect.

In our example, the tilt was that these are parents of spoiled children. The game may be that the children have the run of the house. The mother is a scullery maid to the children, and the father dresses as a clown to entertain them.

The game is a secret weapon in improv, because it allows you to use the clues in front of you to find a through-line to your scene. Here are some examples of games:

- A gung-ho salesman is so customer service-oriented that he eventually gives away the store.
- A Russian cosmonaut is now a New York City cab driver. He super-engineers his cab for high-tech performance, endangering the passengers.

The game becomes important in building written sketches, as discussed later in Section 5.

Practice Spotting the Game

In the middle of an improv, you have so many plates spinning at once that it's hard to spot the game. Review these sets of sparse improvised dialogue and try to identify the game.

> *Player One:* (Laughing) *You always burn your face when you try to light your cigar in the fireplace, Uncle Charlie.*

Player Two: *Ow! Ow! I refuse to use modern technology. Doing it the old fashioned way builds character!*

The game is that Uncle Charlie refuses to use modern conveniences and hurts himself as a result. Players in this scene have it easy — they can iterate instances of the Uncle hurting himself in deference to his low-tech dogma. He generates his own electricity from a treadmill, injuring his back. He whittles a toy for his nephew but slices his hands in the process.

Try this one:

Player One: *Thank God this suntan lotion is SPF 50, Mildred.*
Player Two: *You're so safe, you'll be the one husband of mine who won't ever die — of anything.*

The game is that he's a paranoid third husband and insists on outlandish methods to secure his health. Again, the players in this scene merely need to iterate instances of his safety shenanigans, to the characters' mutual destruction.

Calling the Game
When you think you know the game, state it to the others in the improv in the voice of your character. Use obvious dialogue that boldly identifies the game, so that all players can explore and heighten the game you discovered together. Solidify it.

Player One: *Mother and Father, you care more about my getting into Yale than you do about my ill health!*

Playing the Game
Now that the game is established, add information that supports and furthers the predicament.

Player Two: *Son, we just want to be proud of you! Here's a Yale sweatshirt.*
Player One: *Now there's no room for my medication in my suitcase. I'll die on campus without it!*

Let the game naturally arise from the information you discover together. Allow the newly discovered game to color the new information you add to the scene. Allow the game to *spur you into action* — action that supports the premise. Avoid overlaying a game onto a scene from nowhere. As you develop chemistry with your fellow players, it will become easier to find the game.

Heightening the Game

Once you have called the game, *heighten* the circumstances of your predicament by raising the stakes. That is, pour gasoline on the fire. Make it worse. Intensify the problem.

> **Player One:** Mom and Dad, I feel faint!
> **Player Two:** Son, walk toward the light. Tell God to be good to Yale!
> **Player One:** I'm not dead yet!

Tips

If a player doesn't pick up on the "game" that you identify, it's your fault. Make it clear to them by re-stating the game, as necessary.

Avoid statements like "Calm down." or "It will be okay." If you solve the problem, you will deflate the scene. Heighten the scene by aggravating the problem.

Practice exploring, finding the tilt, growing the game and heightening it by doing the following exercise.

> **"That Means ... "**
>
> In this variation on the "Yes and" exercise, two players substitute "That means ... " for "Yes and" in order to build a premise. Two players sit opposite one another and add information to build a story. Each person responds to the player's previous statement, giving a parallel statement that reinforces and heightens the meaning.
>
> **Player One:** I went to the Yes concert.
> **Player Two:** That means you are a '70s reject.
> **Player One:** That means people laugh at what I wear.
> **Player Two:** That means you wear Superfly clothes.

> *Player One:* That means the crowd made fun of me at the concert.
> *Player Two:* That means they stopped the concert to point you out.
> *Player One:* That means I left the concert in embarrassment.
> *Player Two:* That means when you got to your Volkswagen Beetle
>   in the parking lot, you had four flat tires.

"That Means ... " focuses players on creating a single action together, reinforcing the intended meaning behind the other's statement with an automatic exploring and heightening. Both players agree and build on what the other means. They create patterns of actions, which build a game to the story. (The game in this story is that the '70s nostalgist is justifiably ridiculed for his style.) After you do the "That Means ... " exercise, notice how it influences your scenework. Suddenly you are agreeing, finding a game, and building an absurd world together. This exercise works best if it follows the "Yes and" exercise.

So, the game is the chance to find a through-line and "climb aboard the train" of the scene. At the beginning, watch for a "light to turn on" when you find the tilt, then grow the game together. Create a pattern of behavior based on the game. Instead of trying to find a "conflict" between the two characters that will devolve into an argument, find a game instead.

Inexperienced players sometimes struggle for fifteen minutes and never identify a game as they thrash about the stage. Experienced players can extend the tilt into a game within the first two or three lines of dialogue. Expert players can even find a game with no dialogue at all based on the stage picture or their object work.

Take stock: So, after you have explored, you'll discover a unique pattern, theme, through-line, or gist to your scene, called a

Tips

If a player says "You're hopping mad!," don't start hopping on one foot. Accept the intended meaning — you're angry.

Avoid creating a "plot" in improv. Instead, observe your partner, agree, build the foundation, explore, find a tilt, and grow the game.

game. The game spurs you to action in your scene — action that supports the premise. This is an advanced skill that can take months to develop.

Cleaning Up the Confusing Information

Despite our best efforts to keep an improv setup simple, sometimes scenes get over-complicated and confused because players add contradictory information. Practice clarifying the confusing information and justifying the contradictions. For example, your partner may label you "Uncle," when you already established that you are college roommates. Clear it up with "You sometimes call me 'Uncle' because it's a cool college expression meaning 'friends.' You sure know the lingo!" Or "Yes and" both pieces of information with "It's a little awkward having an uncle as my college roommate, but hey, this is Berkeley — anything goes!"

Tips

Conflict arises naturally from two players with different information merging together. Justifying this accidental incongruity, or tilt, is the root of comedic improv.

If you sense you're nearing the end of an improv and you're looking for an ending, try giving in, or reversing your temperament. "Hey … you might be right for this job after all."

Summary

- *Explore* the environment, emotion, and relationship.
- *Find the tilt* and extend it.
- *Spot the game* and heighten it.
- *Clean up any confusing information* as the scene progresses.

Chapter 12

Basics Wrap-Up

As you progress through your beginning improv class, the number of rules may overwhelm you. Don't worry — the rules become second nature as you develop improv muscle. It takes time.

List of Improv Side-Coaching Phrases

Here are some common phrases you'll hear instructors shout out during improv exercises. Use these coined phrases with your fellow players as you work on improv outside of class. The phrases are like "improv shorthand," allowing you to relay standard criticisms in a succinct, painless way.

- Who are you?
- Where are you?
- Object work!
- Eye contact! Look at your partner!
- Use the fourth wall!
- Use your body!
- Don't negate!
- "Yes and" what your partner just said!
- Label your partner!
- Enter emotionally with object work!
- Don't control your partner!
- Don't plan ahead!
- Tell us why! Justify!
- Change the tempo!
- Don't say "I don't know!"
- No teaching!
- No haggling or bargaining!
- No arguing!
- No questions! Answer it instead!
- You know each other already! Start in the middle of the scene!

- Raise the stakes!
- Change the stage picture!
- Explore and heighten!
- New choice!
- Give in!
- Keep it out of the gutter!
- Become emotional!

Now that you have a groundwork for improv scene work, *practice*. A sample of basic scene exercises appear in the appendix on page 170. There are hundreds more exercises (or *handles* as they are called at some schools). Improv groups create new improv games every week. Consult the Internet for larger lists of performance games and descriptions.

> **Tip**
>
> *With practice, the rules become habitual. You're free to experience the scene.*
>
> *If your scene stagnates, touch your partner. A pat on the back, a handshake, or a hand on the shoulder connects you to your partner, adds new information and advances the scene.*

Take stock: Most students of improv enroll in classes at several schools in order to strengthen their improv skills. Realize that your objective is to build improv muscle and make professional partnerships, not speed through a school's course lineup in hopes of landing a spot in a performance company. The more classes you take, the better off you'll be. The skills you developed in your first class (group mind, rolodexing, agreement, foundation, and game) will be the cornerstones on which you build comic characters in your next class.

Summary

- *Develop a group mind and rolodex information.*
- *Establish the foundation* with dialogue, object work, emotion, stage picture, and character.
- *Agree*, and avoid arguments.
- *Find the game,* and heighten it.
- *Learn the standard side-coaching phrases* and use them as improv "shorthand."

Section 3
Developing Comic Characters

"I usually get a positive response on characters I do in plays, but this is different. This is developing characters from scratch.

It's one thing to develop a character from a playwright's vision, but another thing entirely to write it out of thin air. Now I don't have anyone else to blame if the character doesn't work."

— Author's Journal, December 20, 2001

Chapter 13

Overview

Usually, the "character" class is the second class in an improv school's course lineup. When I started my first character class, I was surprised to find that the approach was "from the outside in." For example, we would often start with a face, a body position, or a label like "Moderate Republican," create the physical and vocal character, and fill in the rest with improv.

How was I supposed to create characters with any depth or breadth if they started from an external impetus? How could I make them real if they're so far from my personal experience? How could I make them funny on the spot? How could I make them last?

The answer didn't come to me until the class was almost over. My most successful comic characters were ones that I could link to my personal character *images* — the snapshots of people's behavior from my life that I had stored in my mind's eye. For example, the way my high school English teacher became so passionate about teaching grammar that he obfuscated the subject beyond recognition, or the way my Uncle Robert laughed at his own jokes so hard he had a heart attack. The images of the people in my life helped create my most human comic characters.

So, the classes use the external to get to the internal. However, it's up to you to take the external character impetuses you're given and connect them to *who you are.*

Get Personal

Your personal experience and imagery are unique, allowing you to create characters with a distinct point of view. Think about the "characters" in your own life — the people who you know or have observed. Ask yourself these questions:

- Who are the characters in my life who have made a strong impression on me?
- Which of the characters capture something about life that is deeply human, ridiculous, painful, or absurd?

Even though most character classes in improv schools emphasize external technique rather than internal discovery, remember to touch base with your wellspring of experience. Make sure that the character rings true to *you*.

Who Are My Models?

When I started on the journey of developing comedic characters, I asked myself the question "Who are my models?" My answer came, "Charlie Chaplin, Buster Keaton, Peter Sellers, Lily Tomlin, Eddie Murphy, and Mike Meyers." These actors created a host of complete, convincing characters, rooted in their personal experiences and observations.

> *Don't become so involved with the technical trappings of voice and body that you forget how this character relates to* you.

They wrote their own material, developed their characters, and revisited them over the course of their careers.

Before you begin, ask yourself about comic characters:

- Which of my model's comic characters resonate with me personally? Why?
- Which comic characters capture a glimpse of humanity — human frailties and triumphs?
- Which comic characters have longevity and durability?

The Class

The character class, often called Intermediate Improv, has spawned many of the recurring characters on *SNL* and *MadTV*, and characters in films like *Wayne's World* and *Austin Powers*.

Institutions like the Gary Austin Workshops, The Groundlings (the comedy institution founded by Austin himself), and ACME Comedy Theater in Los Angeles specialize in the process of creating comedic characters. Austin is known as the father of comedic characters — he studied Spolin's writings, developed character concepts at the Committee, and cultivated character exercises at his own theater, The Groundlings.

In a typical character class, you will create characters through improv, building on the techniques learned in your beginning improv class. You will continue to develop your improv scene skills at an intermediate level, and you'll write monologues — a precursor to writing full-length sketches.

Even if you're not a performer, but a writer, you will benefit from these exercises. You'll learn to assume a voice, rhythm, and point of view — all required skills for creating well-rounded, and even profound, comedic characters.

The Requirements

Creating and developing characters requires intuition, study, practice, and a thick skin. You should have the following requisite skills:

- Basic Improv Skill
- Physical, Vocal, and Emotional Range
- Imitation/Impersonation Skill
- Your Rolodex of Character "Images"

Your success in these classes will fluctuate in any given exercise, depending on your skill level. The strongest characters usually spring forth unexpectedly during improvised monologues or scenes, when you are centered and uninhibited. Stanislavski called it the "creative state," and Spolin called it the "X Area." No matter what the moniker, uninhibited inspiration and connection to yourself give rise to the most deeply human comedic characters.

Some performers say that character building is "too complex and intuitive to document." However, these same performers get stuck when a character is not working. Sure, intuition helps, but guidelines come to the rescue when you need to troubleshoot, or when you need to add range and depth to your characters. Remember, character classes are "hands-on," which is code for "there's no textbook." Again, keep a class journal.

By the end of a character class, you will have amassed at least five workable, fully-drawn comedic characters.

Preparing for Character Exercises

The first thing I did was panic. I created a series of characters and put them on ice, ready to thaw on the first day of class. However, the focus of the class is to create new characters in the moment, without relying on your stock of familiar characters. To prepare for this spontaneous feat, strengthen the tools in your tool belt by doing the following exercises outside of class:

- *Exercise your range of expression,* both physical and vocal. Play with *adjustments*, which are changes in character essence, like posture, physical appearance, accents, speech patterns, attitudes, points of view, and language.
- *Develop single syllable expressions* for character faces you create, like "Hmph!" or "Mmmmm!" Repeat the expression, varying it slightly, until the character comes to life and speaks.
- *Work from the outside in,* using a mirror, masks, costume pieces, and wigs. Even though you won't improvise with props and costumes in class, this gets the creative juices flowing.
- *Work from the inside out,* exploring the attitudes, emotions, and images of characters from your life experience. These images are uniquely yours. They are your comic wellspring.

In preparation for your class, use the following exercise to start from character "square one."

65

Mood Swing (a.k.a. *Random Emotions*)

In this solo character preparation exercise outside of class, sit in a chair across from a mirror. Begin telling a story about your most recent vacation. Speak as yourself, and retell the incidents of the vacation as if talking to a friend in a manner that is natural and genuine. During the story, intermittently open pieces of paper with an emotion pre-written on each. Transition from the old emotion and adopt each new emotion as you continue your story.

Assume the emotions honestly and energetically, transitioning between the opposite emotions gradually and convincingly. Open six or seven pieces of paper, each with an emotion, during the two-minute story. Each time you adjust to a new random emotion, you must justify it in your story. Finally, when the pieces of paper run out, recover to the neutral state in which you began, and complete the story.

The focus of the exercise is the exploration of simple emotions while speaking. You play yourself and allow the emotions to become intense while remaining honest. Allow the emotion to affect the content of your story.

At the end, you come full circle with the emotions, coming back to the original state in which you began as if nothing happened. (Returning to an original state after an ordeal is a classic structural component in comedy scenes, providing a clean, satisfying ending based on repetition.)

Emotions change the "details" of a story. Emotions bend the truth and establish a *point of view* — the set of values that comprise character. Emotions are the actor's anchor.

The more you prepare with exercises like this one, the stronger your "plunge" into characters will become.

Tip

Make a conscious effort to observe the people in your life — their expressions, attitudes, and flaws. Build a library of character traits.

The four chapters that follow will help you build strong comic characters:

- Developing Character Essences
- The Character Toolbox
- Character Workout
- Celebrity Impersonations

Chapter 14

Developing Character Essences

Most comic characters, even complex characters, start as an *essence*.

Character essence (or character "shell") is simply the *look, sound,* and *game* of your character: the posture, the facial expressions, the pitch and tone of the voice, the mannerisms, attitude, and patterns of behavior — *everything but the life details*.

Later, you will add detail and complexity to these character essences by applying tools from your character tool belt, by improvising with the characters, and by writing monologues and scenes for them. Eventually, these characters may become recurring characters in sketch shows or the subjects of full-length feature films.

First, start with the essence. The best place to discover character essence is in solo exercises.

> *"When I 'take the plunge' into a brand new character*
> *essence in front of everybody, it feels like I'm taking a big,*
> *fat risk with only a one in ten chance of it paying off.*
> *But, when it pays off, it pays off big. I just*
> *created a spontaneous, authentic character that*
> *I may work with for the rest of my life. The other*
> *nine essences I created tonight? Don't ask."*
> *— Author's Journal, January 7, 2002*

The Format for Most Solo Character Exercises

The character-building exercises usually follow this pattern:

1. *Suggestion.* The director gives a suggestion as a starting point: an expression, a place, a posture, a musical instrument, etc.

2. *Rolodex.* Intuitively scan through your personal experience, observations of human irony, and your character "images." Your character *images* are the snapshots of people's behavior that you have stored in your mind's eye. For example, your aunt's fearless attitude toward death, or the way the barista at your Starbucks has a high-pitched voice and an inferiority complex.

3. *"Take the Plunge."* Spontaneously dive into a physical and vocal persona based on the suggestion. The more flexible you are physically and vocally, the more distinct your character will be.

4. *Foundation.* Discover the foundation of the scene: who the character is, where he is, the activity (the what), and his emotion. Acknowledge each spontaneous piece of information, letting the character take shape without interference.

5. *Game.* Explore and heighten a game (pattern) in the character's behavior or circumstance.

6. *Finish/Assess.* The instructor determines a cutoff point, based on the natural progression of the scene, generally after three to five minutes. Then, you and the instructor determine how the character can be developed further.

> *"I'm nervous about my characters bombing.*
> *I don't want the instructor to think I'm not funny.*
> *I am going to stop experimenting so much with new*
> *character essences in class. Instead I'll use old essences I*
> *know already. It's less risky."*
> — *Author's Journal, January 12, 2002*

Taking the Plunge

Try the following simple character essence exercise using the character exercise format.

Giants (a.k.a. *Character Walk, Spolin's Space Walk/Attitude*)

This exercise, originated by Spolin and developed by Gary Austin of The Groundlings, is done individually. Walk randomly around the stage. The instructor calls out a single character or celebrity (e.g., "defense attorney" or "Pope"). Assume the physicality of the character, based on your personal images. As you discover the character's walk, begin to speak as the character, and play the given character *large* — with utter commitment, finding a heightened emotion. You are a giant version of this character. Remember to create object work that is *specific* and germane to the environment of that character (not just gestures). Allow the object work to influence your specific, heightened emotion or attitude. This exercise demonstrates that you can generate characters from nothing more than a given character credential, physicality, object work, and a resulting emotion.

Here's a simple example:

Godzilla: (Angrily holding his foot.) *No one makes shoes big enough for me! I've got a lot of stomping to do, and my exoskeleton doesn't cover my feet. Get Dr. Scholl in here, A-SAP!*

This simple improv demonstrates that comic essences spring forth naturally from the information around you — your object work, emotion, voice, and body. Once you set up these details, all you do is react, and the character is born.

Your character springs forth from *you*, or an aspect of you, doing *this* task (object work), with *this* emotion, in *this* environment. Your personal insecurities are the character's insecurities. Your emotion is the character's emotion. Don't hold back. This exercise is your chance for unbridled experimentation. This is where you stretch your character range. This is where you'll find character gold. However, you will have to risk failing in front of everyone in order to find it.

Take stock: How did you do? Did you allow your voice and body to adapt to the given suggestion? Did you nervously return to "that place you go" — a familiar character you do when you're stressed? Did you add lots of specific information about your predicament? Did you avoid questions? Did you avoid *"I don't know ... "* and *"I'm not sure ... "*? Did your emotion heighten the stakes and root your character in a specific intention? Was it easy for you to find specific object work for the character? Did the object work help define your character's environment? Were you playful and flexible, or nervous and tense? Practice these exercises outside of class to become comfortable with "taking the plunge."

Exercises
"Taking the Plunge" into Character Essences
The exercises in the appendix on page 172 will allow you to practice discovering physical and vocal personae with specific points of view. You'll develop characters in the moment, based on the scene requirements.

Building Characters from a Random Suggestion
In the exercises listed in the appendix on page 173, you create characters based on random "ask fors." You create the character's game around that given information. The secret in these exercises is to develop an emotional point of view stemming from the character's environment, emotion, and activity.

Building Characters from an Exaggerated Trait
The Church Lady, a Dana Carvey character on *SNL*, invited guests to her talk show only to cast moral judgment on them. She repressed her vicarious enjoyment of their sins. Practice developing characters from an exaggerated trait using the exercises detailed in the appendix section called Character Exercises on page 174.

Tips

> *Pump up a flat character by adding an unlikely emotion or an attribute (e.g., age, sexiness, innocence, ego, or stealth). For example, adding "horny" to an egghead computer geek makes him more complex — and more pathetic.*
>
> *Usually company members have three to six characters ready to use. Three are on the "tip of their tongue."*

The Leading Authority (a.k.a. *Expert Talker*)

In this solo improv, developed by Gary Austin, the instructor assigns a player the character of a specialist in a given field, like "motocross course designer." The character talks confidently, knowledgeably, and emotionally about his complex topic, as if giving a speech at a seminar. The player adds a who, what, where, and object work. After the three-minute informational speech, the instructor opens the floor to questions from the other players in the audience.

The key to this exercise is the universal human truth that no matter how expert someone is, their expertise is tainted by their personality — their character flaws, their point of view, and their emotions.

In addition, there's humor in seeing a player struggle to provide information on an unfamiliar, complex topic. Because the odds are stacked so high against the player, character irony bubbles out instinctively. The player is lying about his knowledge, providing a ready-made character flaw — the character is fibbing about his expertise. This is most players' first taste of playing a character irony.

Rehearse this exercise outside of class. Think of absurd topics, and "take the plunge" into a persona with a character flaw. Ask yourself impossible questions and answer them with utter commitment, adding specific information about your specialty. The more you practice, the easier it is to create character ironies or games for any given suggestion. Here are some examples:

Furniture Maker: I'll show you how to judge the construction and design of a good couch. I take this science very seriously at Omaha ComfortTech. (He sits.) Ohhhh, now this is a good couch. You have to sit in them two or three hours to get a real handle on assessing the quality of construction of one of these babies. I might just put this couch on my list of nominees for a Furniture Construction Award. We call them the "Cushies." But, it takes weeks to judge ...

Film Score Composer: Frankly, I am holding this film score seminar because I haven't sold any music since my divorce. The market is soft. I want to introduce my most recent musical composition, and here it is. Boom! Boom! The tympani comes in **angry**, like your wife just filed for divorce. Then the **crash** of the cymbals like you've been served a restraining order, and the low brass comes in like (Singing ominously) you just lost custody of your kid ...

Take stock: How did you do? I was nervous both times I did this exercise in class. The second time, I was handed a topic that threw me. When the instructor assigned the character "Ergonomics Engineer," I thought, "Now what in Dayton can I do with *that*?" The only game I managed to eek out of the character was that he repeatedly insulted the assembled audience. After the exercise, I thought of a million things I could have done.

I could have offered a ton of unique "information" on the topic (the way neo-scientists do). I could have discovered a character game (like an obsession with my own posture). I could have been more clear in the setup of the foundation — who (ergo engineer), what (frustrated with the chair they provided me), and where (ergonomics conference). I could have used object work (like a ridiculously over-mechanized, ergonomically correct chalkboard). I could have become intensely emotional about the topic. Hindsight is always 20/20. Nevertheless, the more I thought about the approach, the more prepared I was for next time.

Maximize Your Solo Exercises

Here are some tips that help you in solo exercises and keep you from singing the "Coulda Shoulda Blues":

> *"I can't think of anything funny to say in solo scenes. I feel boxed in to the dull suggestion the instructor gives me."*
> — *Author's Journal, May 3, 2001*

- *Be specific.* Add detail. Because the topics are general, the comedy comes from the detail you add to it. Example: If you're given the title "Juvenile Delinquent," add to it that you are an Internet hacker making three million dollars a year online while in juvenile detention. Develop opinions about the specific type of items you work with (e.g., my Palm Pilot, my "blog"). Specify who you are, who the audience is, where you are, and why you've convened here. Develop an emotional, intense point of view.

Tips

If an improv bombs, you can take away from it the victory that you remained committed to your character.

Make high-stakes choices. Avoid wimps, mutes, and wallflower characters who withhold information.

- *Use the audience.* In the Leading Authority scenes, interact with the audience members. Develop a bias for some and a hatred for others — public speakers aren't immune to these flaws.
- *Rolodex* the interesting information you know about the topic. If you're an air conditioning repair specialist, talk about hiding in the ducts and putting amyl nitrate in the ventilation system a la Studio 54. Think crime, fantasy, and adventure.
- *Use your object work and stage picture.* How does the character deal with his props and environment? Maybe he's upset that his exhibits were set up incorrectly, or he's astonished at the high-tech presentation equipment. The character's attitude toward the minutiae of the demonstration is what reveals the character's irony.

- *Get to the fun part.* In the speech, we want to see the character dance, sing, or demonstrate shimmying down an HVAC duct. Don't "save the show for later." Show us whatever is most physical, entertaining, vulnerable, embarrassing, or universally human.
- *Avoid the cliché.* Develop characters that are different than your fellow players' characters. Cloistered suburban mothers and flamboyant hairdressers are always in plentiful supply. Go beyond the boundaries of what feels safe and familiar. Select foundation information that is fresh and original.

Allow your unique point of view to color your character. If technical jargon isn't your strong suit, leap anyway. Incorporate the flaw into your character.

Take stock: You may have found several character essences that you like to play, and that your classmates like to watch. Now, learn how to add depth and complexity to your character essences.

Summary
- *Character essence is the character's look, sound, and game.*
- *Taking the plunge feels awkward.* Arm yourself.
- *Heighten the character* by receiving the suggestion, rolodexing, taking the physical and vocal plunge, building the foundation, building a game, and getting feedback.
- *Challenge yourself.* Go beyond what feels safe.

Chapter 15

The Character Toolbox

Once you have created character essences, you can begin to add detail using the character toolbox. These methods strengthen your ability to create and sustain characters, both in improvised scenes and in written sketches:

- Building Character History
- Building Character Game
- The Longevity Test
- Character Psychology 101
- Labeling Your Partner

Comic characters that stand the test of time have depth and changeability — depth to make them real, and changeability to make them usable in any scenario.

Building Character History

To add depth to a character, research the details of his life. To increase the changeability of a character, practice playing with his *demographics* — or life statistics.

> *"I have lots of character impressions of people from work and stuff, but they're only funny in the context that they came from. How can I make them work anywhere?"*
> *— Author's Journal, December 22, 2001*

For example, practice changing your character's job — does the character's game work when he's a recycling center attendant or an inept ballet dancer? Practice "coloring" your character with specific demographic attributes. Keep the essence (the look, sound, and game of the character) the same.

Outside of class, select a character and improvise a monologue in front of a mirror. Tweak your character by modifying his various character attributes. Record the attributes that work best:

- **Demographics** — age, background, education, geographic location, family, children, ethnicity, job, social status, financial status, police record, awards, travel, languages, etc.
- **Psychographics** — political party, sexual orientation, spirituality, aspirations, cultural interests, charitable giving, memberships in organizations, volunteer associations, spending habits, sociability, etc.
- **Miscellaneous** — preferred books, newspapers, magazines, TV stations, radio stations, pets, restaurants, clothing styles, foods, music, film, computer aptitude, etc.

Does your character's essence survive when you change him demographically? Which attributes heighten the character? Keep the attributes that work and discard the ones that don't.

The more you play with your character's demographics, the more ready the character is for *anything* — improvised monologues, two-person scenes, and even written sketches. Each time you bring your character essence back to an interview, you add material. You add depth and flexibility to the character. When you bring a character back for a second interview, strike a balance between the prepared material and improvised exploration.

Tip

> Once you create your character essence (the look, feel, and game of the character), you can change the character's demographic to suit any scene, keeping his essence intact.

Building Character Game

Just as improvised scenes capture a game (a scenic theme or gist), your comic characters capture a game, too. Jon Lovitz's Tommy Flanagan blatantly lies again and again, but thinks he succeeds. ("I dated Morgan Fairchild. Yeah ... that's the ticket!") Tommy Flanagan's game adheres to several guidelines:

- *The character has a universally human flaw* (e.g., lying to gain social status).

- *The character's game is repeatable* inside the structure of the sketch.
- *The character's game is usable in any scene,* and goes beyond a single prop or gimmick.
- *The character's game is linked to a "hook"* (e.g., "We're two wild and crazy guys!").
- *The character is unaware of his problem.*

Character games become easier to find the more characters you create. At first, more obvious games like pathological lying give way to less common ones, like a needy teenager steeped in sarcasm until she needs to borrow the car keys; or a pious priest who warns against the seven deadly sins, but indulges in lengthy ruminations on each one.

The Longevity Test

Here's the test to determine if your character is a flexible character ready for any scene, or a Johnny One-note tied to a gimmick. Improvise a series of scenes with the character. Does his game survive? (For example, a meter maid who receives harsh treatment from auto owners isn't a universally ironic quality that could live outside a parking scenario. But a controlling woman on a power trip, one who dominates others as a way to compensate for her lack of social status, could easily live in any scenario you place her — from Stonehenge to Versailles.)

Cultivate universal irony, not just character traits that are dependent on a scene gimmick or a "where." Your objective is to tie your character to universal human behavior, so that your characters have long-term potential for additional scenes and feature film.

Develop your character's longevity by asking the following questions:

- *What truth is the character hiding?*
- *How does the character use his facade* to hide this unbearable truth?
- *How do others treat the character* because of his flaw?
- *How does the character demonstrate his flaw* with colorful examples?

Character Psychology 101

Drop hints as to the reason why your character behaves the way he does. Let the audience play psychoanalyst; let them in on the joke. The audience is searching for the origin of the character's flaw. Let your character tell them, without allowing the character to figure it out for himself.

So, if you're just playing the given attribute "efficient" without revealing hints as to why you are this way, there's no payoff. There's no logical background. Drop subtle hints as to the reasons for this character's point of view. ("Some of you need a good efficiency lesson. It's called the Depression. I lived through it and you will too — today in this seminar!")

Let the audience "ride with you" as the character struggles with his flaw. They'll know more than the character does about himself, and enjoy the irony. Remember, if characters knew their problems, they would fix them. So, avoid qualifying statements like "I know I'm a little weird" and "I know this sounds crazy ... " The character doesn't know.

As you look at the following examples of character games, practice playing a given attribute like "bitter" and adding information to it. Practice developing a game from it. Practice writing dialogue that reveals the "why" about a character's game (without the character recognizing it himself).

So, it's not enough just to play "bitter." We need to know the background. We want to see examples. We want to understand the why.

Given Attribute	Develop a Game	Show It in Dialogue
Bitter (An emotion)	She is bitter about her difficult childhood, but covers it up with a high-powered career.	"Happy young women grow up to be weak. But, focused young women like me grow up to be leaders! For example, I never had a slumber party, now I'm a CEO. It's a small price to pay for greatness."
Hunchback (A physical attribute the character can't help)	He compensates for his misery by saying he likes it that way.	"I'm proud of my being a hunchback. Makes me unique. I'm gonna find a wife who looks like a lower case letter r. And we'll have letter-r children, dammit."
Bodybuilder (A self-imposed physical state)	He claims to be an athlete, but really wants revenge on high school bullies.	"I'm number one in my weight class. My trophy could probably crush certain people — certain people who were mean to me at one time in high school. But, I would never let that happen. I'm above that."
Life of the party (A desirable attribute)	She is concealing the pain of recent divorce.	"Free again! Lucky LUCKY me, I'm free again! I can party 'til dawn because my husband doesn't care about me any more! Par-tay!"
Policeman (A credential)	He wants revenge on people who are smarter than he is.	"Step out of the car Mr. Harvard yacht club! Mr. 1600 on the SAT! It's time to pay the piper!"
Napoleonic complex (A psychological condition)	He is covering up physical inadequacies.	"It's not physical size that matters. It's your spiritual size. That's why I'm a Promise Keeper."

Defense Mechanisms

To help you create your character's game, try adopting one or more of these defense mechanisms. (There are more listed here than you'll be able to take in. Start with the one that catches your eye.)

- **Behave altruistically.** Excessively help others, to the point of hurting yourself.
- **Compartmentalize** by separating your questionable behavior, justifying it, and guarding it from criticism.
- **Compensate** for your weaknesses by emphasizing strength in other areas.
- **Deny** reality as a way to avoid painful thoughts or feelings.
- **Develop a "reaction formation."** Hide your flaw by assuming an opposite attitude or action.
- **Develop a phobia** or an irrational fear of an unlikely future event.
- **Displace** your emotion about your problem onto those who have nothing to do with it.
- **Exaggerate** an attribute to absurd proportions. Make the dominant physical trait your "big issue."
- **Fantasize** success in other settings, so you can ease the pain of criticism.
- **Fixate** on a past incident that influenced your mindset.
- **Intellectualize** your problem, avoiding emotional involvement.
- **Project** your own problem onto others.
- **Rationalize** and justify an unacceptable outcome.
- **Regress** to an earlier stage of development as a way to deal with your fears.
- **Repress** your underlying feelings about what you really want to be.
- **Sublimate** by channeling your bad behavior into socially acceptable outlets; i.e., screaming at an umpire.
- **Be Type A** by focusing on action, impatience, success, and extreme competition.
- **Be Type B** by focusing on inaction, relaxation, and minimal competition.
- **Undo your bad behavior** by excessively doing the opposite.

Now practice creating a character from a given attribute. Your objective is to receive a suggestion, add information to it, develop a game, and show it in dialogue.

> **Characters from Animal Spines or Household Objects**
> Group. In this exercise based on Spolin's "Animal Images," players walk randomly around the stage. The instructor calls out a suggestion: an object or an animal. Players first physically transform into the essence of the animal or object. Then players morph into a walking, talking character. The character is human, but retains the attributes of their object or animal. Players should set up the foundation, become emotional, and use their bodies. Any impetus (animals, appliances, books) can be the starting point for a character. Players briefly interact with others in the group. The focus in this exercise is developing complete character essence — physical and vocal — and developing a point of view.

Tips

Sometimes a whole character can stem from a single physical attribute.

Remember to delete your own personal attributes from a character's essence, like the way you adjust your glasses or your speaking rhythm.

Labeling Your Partner

Labeling is a standard routine in improv where players describe each other for comic effect.

Player One: *Mr. O'Leary, you're a grumpy, womanizing Supreme Court Justice, spitting tobacco wherever you please!*

In improv, when you label your partner like this, because of the rule of agreement, you oblige your partner to behave as described. When the player performs the traits that you set up, there's an instant payoff for the audience. Labels can be emotions (e.g., grumpy), psycho/socio/physical attributes (e.g., womanizing) or credentials (e.g., Supreme Court Justice). Even a character's name can be a potential attribute (e.g., O'Leary). Sometimes the director labels characters *before* the scene starts as part of the scene structure. Sometimes players label each other *during* the scene.

For practice, write a list of related character attributes, e.g., "suicidal," "backstabbing," "curious," and "randy." Write a list of character credentials, e.g., "priest," "pauper," and "swindler." Practice adopting these attributes in monologues you do outside of class. Emotions, attributes, and credentials all have the same effect in improv — they help you develop a character point of view, which advances the scene.

In improvs where the instructor labels the players before the improv starts, you must remember your own label, and your partners', too. During the improvised scene, *set up* (provide opportunity for) each player so they can *pay off* (exhibit) his or her assigned traits. In other words, *trigger your partner to do his shtick.* Your partners will do the same for you. Simple traits are easy to set up; complex traits

> ## Tip
>
> Avoid "pimping" your fellow players. Pimping is labeling your partners with undesirable character traits to see them struggle.

are harder — you have to give that player extra attention. For example, if your partner has a label of "technophobe," hand him a cell phone during an emergency, or mock him because he was afraid to use the doorbell. Label the players you know well with attributes you know they like to play.

Some scenes require you to set up a third player who waits offstage. Be sure to wait until *after* you completely establish the scene to label his character. Don't even think about introducing another character offstage until you know who *you* are, where you are, or what you're doing. The character enters emotionally, with object work, and embodies the attributes you gave him. He pays off the attributes you set up and furthers the game in the scene.

Exercises — Building Characters from Labels

To help you learn to set up and pay off character attributes in improv using labels, use the exercises shown in the appendix, page 176. (Labeling helps set up characters efficiently in written sketches, too.)

Tips

In improvs with three or more players, you can enter and exit the scene, bringing on new information to keep the scene moving.

In monologue exercises, focus your character on a single problem. Too many intentions confuse the main thrust of a character.

If your scene gets stagnant, make a bold choice. Leap and the net will appear. Discover a nude picture (object work), become giddy (add emotion), or collapse (change the stage picture). Your partner should help you justify your new choice based on what you know already in the scene.

Helpful Hints

Avoiding Easy Targets

Avoid playing cliché character traits like "old" or "disabled." Instead, lampoon the character's ridiculous hubris and flaws. For example, if you must lampoon an "old man," make him an insatiable thrill-seeker and self-avowed "stuntman." An obsessed geriatric stuntman who puts himself at risk deserves to be lampooned.

Avoid cruel, kick-the-dog humor targeting disease or disability that are out of the character's control. After all, in this era, "old" isn't old anymore; seventy is young. Wheelchairs are cool. When you do a disabled character, give him self-imposed personality flaws, and then skewer him to your heart's content.

Keepin' It Real

You can heighten characters exponentially as long as they are believable, convincing, and not "put on." You can avoid "crossing the line" of believability if you develop specific intentions, commit truthfully, and develop a cohesive logic to the character. Martin Short's "Jiminy Glick" is almost over the top, but the actor keeps it real. He employs specific intentions, remains fully committed, and creates a logical world of absurdity. As a result, Jiminy is an utterly convincing character, even though he's larger than life.

Take stock: So far, you've created a couple of simple characters using the basic object work and emotion exercise. You've reviewed building a character's history to give him depth. You've reviewed how to build your character's game, and used the longevity test to determine if your character can live past the current scene. You have explored the common psychological defense mechanisms and learned how to use labels. Now, using these tools, give your characters a workout, in solo, two-person, and three-person scenes.

Summary

- *Create characters from any impetus,* as long as you have a strong opinion about it.
- *Build your character's history, game, and longevity.*
- *Explore your character's psychology.*
- *Use labels* to establish characters in improvs.

Chapter 16

Character Workout

So far, you have taken the plunge into character essences and added character detail using the character "toolbox."

Now, practice all these skills at once by improvising and writing a free-form monologue, prepared on your own, outside of class. "Take the plunge" into a character essence, establish the foundation (who, what, and where), become emotional, and build a character game. As you improvise with this character outside of class, transcribe what you say in your improvised monologue, type it up, and memorize it. Don't worry about writing technique now. It is covered later in the chapter called "Writing Sketch Comedy."

Internet Character

The instructor assigns you a character you find on an Internet website. Internet Weblogs, or "blogs," often reveal personal information about real people and are great character starters. Select a character from a personal Internet website — one that is not your normal surfing ground, e.g., a "Teamster" or a "Raisin Bargaining Coalition Member." Outside of class, you will prepare a character and a free-form monologue. Then, in the next class session, you will perform your monologue. (Start with the standard approach: rolodex, "take the plunge" into the character essence, develop the foundation, grow the character game, explore the character's history and defense mechanisms.)

Later in the class session, the instructor uses the same characters from the Internet Character exercise in two-person improvised scenes with a given "where" and "what." The two-person scene challenges you to hold on to the character essence from the Internet Character exercise. You must *retain*

> the character's mannerisms, attitudes, and games, but *change* his demographic slightly to fit the two-person scene.
>
> To help you with the Internet Character exercise, develop your character's jargon.

Developing Your Character's Lingo

When you develop a character's history and establish his demographic makeup, create the character's vocabulary. In creating an Internet Character, a grunge rocker I named Joshua Wortek, I searched the Internet for his expressions, using general search words like "grunge rock lingo" and "grunge jargon." The search results were varied, from interviews to translation dictionaries, but it all helped to create a rolodex of the character's information.

Assemble the random vocabulary from your search results in a list:

Moist shock, moist effluvium, "Eyeless in Gaza," cars washing up on shore, dead band members, arena versus "econo-rock," capitalist under-belly of rock, don't "ghettoize" me, James Joyce's *Ulysses*, Dante's *Inferno*, putting people in places where they can't hear any sound because they're so far away, overpriced tickets, "merchandising is out of this world," dead earth, freaking brisk, Ambient Lice, wicked, bribing a DJ at a rock station to play the album.

The vocabulary gave me clues to developing a character game. Here is an example of my finished monologue from the "Internet Character" exercise:

Joshua: (Furtively) *You're doing a killer job as agent for our band, Ambient Lice, but I'm here on a secret mission. Ambient Lice is all about econo-rock, playing small clubs and such. But, now that we're getting hot in Seattle, we can play some arenas and appear in a Nintendo game and such. Nkay? I mean, Nintendo! That would be moist!*

Hey, if my selling out ever gets out of this room, we're screwed! If you tell the other guys that I said anything about making money, my rep is down the tubes, so don't fist me on this Jeff.

I'm all about Ambient Lice, I'm into the band, totally ... But, (secretively) *I want to go solo, "Joshua Wortek and the Socratic Shepherds," and such, nkay? My father is putting serious onerous pressure on me and the guys in the band to make some money. I want to show my paternal unit that he doesn't own me, and that I can make it big and shove fistfuls of dough in his cakehole. We need arena cash flow. For once I want to have some success that my old man doesn't own.* (Slurps his own spit and cries.)

To be honest, the band has been living off my dad for the past year or so. He even paid for the funerals of the two band members we lost in separate accidents. Jeremy froze to death while visiting his parents in Saskatoon, and Borneo smashed his van into a tanker on the wicked curve outside of Seattle. Do you know what that's like to ask your dad to pay for two band member funerals in the same week? I'm hurting about losing those two guys. But I found two other dudes who fit in real well with the group, and I'm ready to move on.

Also, Tyler's been getting on my last white nerve because he's taking lead vocals away from me. Nkay? You need to press down hard on this kid, an tell him to step back, nkay? (Slurp.)

Keep it quiet, but my father has some money, and he told me to tell you that it would be in your best interest, nkay?, to... receive the money ... nkay? ... in exchange for coming down hard on Tyler, and making my picture bigger, everywhere. I think it's in the best interest of the band. So, not that I care, but ... what will it be, sir?

As you can see, the monologue incorporated some of the jargon I found on the Internet search and helped me develop the character's game — he's an antiestablishment grunge rocker on the outside, and a capitalist pig on the inside.

88

Here's the brief instructor feedback on my prepared character interview:

Instructor's Feedback

- Fun character with an identifiable irony — he's a grunge rocker who is really a capitalist, underneath it all.
- The rocker deaths should tie in better with their careers, not unrelated accidents.
- Keep your voice in the upper range.
- Repeat your hook phrase, "'nkay? 'nsuch" throughout, not just at the end.
- Later, when you improvised in a scene, you suddenly abandoned your established mannerisms and expressions.

Instructor notes address everything from the conceptual to the technical: voice, posture, foundation, character game, and your skill in placing a fleshed-out character in improvised scenes.

Tips

You only need a couple of unique rolodexed items to infuse a scene with interesting information.

Monologues require foundational elements: who, what, where, object work, tempo changes, emotion and point of view. Without the continual adding of new information, the scene dies.

Classic Character Exercises

Solo Exercises — Characters from People You Know

The exercises in this section help you create characters from familiar people whom you've observed closely. Remember, you're not doing "impersonations." Instead, you are searching your "card catalogue" of character flaws and heightening those flaws. You've done all the prep work already — you've already built a library of images, the character's personal ironies, the lies, the character flaws, and points of view. After you try these solo exercises, use your character in two-person scenes — improvised *and* written. Notice how your fleshed-out character adds incredible momentum and a host of specific information to your improvised scenes.

Don't forget your character's expressions and physicalization now that you're in the middle of an improv. Keep all the plates spinning at once.

Tips

Is your character a friend or foe? Does your character have charisma or "horrisma?" Reveal immediately whether or not you're a protagonist or antagonist in your monologue's first few lines. Once the audience knows, they'll "ride with you."

Flesh out the character by building from the list of demographic attributes, like favorite color, pets, etc.

A "hook" is a telling expression that repeats throughout the character's speech. A hook can provide a recurring pattern and understructure for your sketch.

Even though some character exercises begin in a chair, be sure to develop a complete physicalization — posture, walk, tempo, rhythm, and style of movement.

Make your character vulnerable and human. The audience identifies with characters who have flaws.

Your Grade School Teacher

In this character exercise in use at The Groundlings, create a character based on a quirky teacher or coach that you had when you were growing up and write a free-form, three-minute monologue. Then, memorize it for a class performance.

Begin by distilling the essence of this person, based on your childhood knowledge of them. You know this person well and can harvest the character ironies easily, (e.g., their emotional weakness for Fleetwood Mac songs, their hidden fear of getting older, or their *Star Trek* fantasy.) Heighten all the teacher's characteristics to absurd proportions. Exaggerate his flaws. Don't worry about writing technique. Structure and form aren't important now. Instead, talk extemporaneously as this new character performing an activity outside the classroom. (Avoid teaching.) Write down everything you say. Who are you? Where are you? What are you doing right now? What's on your mind?

Heighten the stakes by becoming emotionally involved in your current circumstances.

Make today the "big day" when you make a realization or you achieve an objective that launches your specific, emotional reaction. The big day doesn't have to be a wedding, Bat Mitzvah, or the Pope coming to town. Your big day can matter to you, and you alone. For example, maybe you are scared to ask a coworker on a date, or you are desperately worried you have some food stuck in your teeth. Avoid expressions like "Whatever," "Who cares?" and "Same old, same old."

After you perform the monologue, the instructor "workshops" your character by asking impromptu interview questions, coaching you, and giving you *adjustments* — which are recommended changes to your physical and vocal mannerisms. Have a strong opinion on every question. Incorporate your instructor's feedback as you speak. Try adding your instructor's recommended mannerisms to the mix.

Take Stock: Were you able to incorporate your instructor's feedback during your interview? When the instructor asked you a yes/no question, did you boldly answer "yes" in order to discover something new? Did you allow your emotions to take you to a place you didn't plan to go? Which of your *planned* games and expressions elicited a strong response from your classmates? Which of them fell flat? Which of your *newly discovered* expressions and mannerisms support your character's game? If you were to bring that character back again, which aspects would you keep? Which aspects would you discard? Is this a strong enough character for you to consider including in your "final five" characters at the end of class?

Characters from Scratch

It's a little tougher to create characters who aren't based on a real person. You'll have to mix and match attributes from any source you can find. Your sources include your rolodex of observed behaviors, your personal images and experiences, and even new discoveries in front of a mirror.

Make an effort to fully explore your characters' points of view and mannerisms. It takes time alone in front of a full-length mirror or video camera, repeating expressions and building a library of character essences, character games, and character histories.

Here are some basic guidelines for creating characters from people who don't exist:

- *Make high percentage choices* about your character. Make them intelligent, opinionated, and emotional, with a specific point of view.

- *Differentiate your characters.* Display your range of physical and vocal traits.

- *Try splicing characteristics* from two characters into one, e.g., overlaying a previously created "sexy woman" on top of a "devout vegan" creates instant duality. She claims to be a vegetable biologist, but underneath it all, she's really a sexpot who lives in an SUV.

- *Make sure we know your character's demographics* by the end of your monologue or interview (who you are, where you work, your age, your income level, your education, etc.). The more we know about your background, the more we can "ride with you."

- *Make your character active, not passive.* Be the instigator of an incident, not the victim of it. (Don't be a mistreated secretary on National Secretary's Day, be the boss.) Avoid being the "unfortunate recipient" of an incident (e.g., a ghost

> ## Tips
>
> *In three-person scenes, pick a side. Don't play negotiator. Don't be neutral.*
>
> *In improv, you're allowed to modify your object work slightly to fit the other player's object work. Otherwise, you'll have to justify why your activity differs.*
>
> *In two-person scenes, don't talk to "space people" (imaginary characters who aren't in the scene).*
>
> *Make the scene about your partner. Avoid talking about characters who will never appear. Instead of "I had a date with this girl who treated me badly," it should be "YOU treated me badly on our date."*

appears in a house that you're buying). Instead, be the doer with a proactive intention. Be the archer, not the target. Be the flawed sinner, not the absolver.

Bringing Your Prepared Characters to a Two-Person Improv

When you improvise using a prepared character, you deal with a new set of challenges:

- *Don't forget the standard improv tools* now that you're in a character-based scene (who, what, where, object work, change the tempo, add emotion, change the stage picture, and "Yes and" your partner).

- *Don't drop the character* now that you're in an improv. You're likely to drop the character and return to "that place you go" when you're in the heat of the improv.

- *Don't let denials creep in* when you improvise with your prepared character. You're more inclined to say "no" to an offer because it goes against your prepared information. Instead, adapt to the new premise and justify your saying "yes."

- *Bring your character's essence (his expressions and games) to the improv,* and change his demographics to fit the scene.

Tips

Even in advanced improvs, start the scene by observing your partner and doing silent object work for seven seconds.

Avoid commenting on the improv, which is to remark, as an actor, on the improv in progress. Stay true to the character in the scene.

In prepared monologues, use the fourth wall and address your invisible partner. Avoid having a back and forth conversation — we can't hear your imaginary partner's dialogue.

Exercises — Using Characters in Improvised Scenes

The advanced practice exercises in the appendix on page 176 help you keep your improv skills sharp: foundation, rolodexing, becoming emotional, exploring object work, adding character, and using a unique stage picture.

Your Character Class "Final Exam"

At the end of the course, this advanced improv challenges you to display the collection of contrasting characters you've developed in class:

Character Party

All players. In this casual exercise at the end of a character class, all players assemble in a room for a real end-of-class party, with a twist. At the instructor's command, all players become a character that they have developed during the course. Characters casually interact with one another and play off of each other's emotions. (Players should concentrate on interacting with one player at a time as they roam through the party.) After five or ten minutes, at the instructor's command, all players become a second character, continuing the party. This exercise works best if players already know each other's characters, jumping into the middle of the conversation, avoiding slow and painstaking introductions. Players are free to become emotional and must be aware of the give and take of conversation. After the players have done their cache of characters, the instructor asks the players to recount interesting interactions, mining the conversations for possible sketches. (Focus: character history, emotions, listening, continuity, character range.)

Consider these points as you select and prepare your characters for the exercise. Make sure your characters have the following:

- *Physical and vocal uniqueness.* Contrast your characters. Make each character unlike your own demeanor and different from fellow players' characters.
- *A range of emotions.*
- *A universally human character flaw* that he doesn't know about, otherwise he'd change.
- *A series of games* to play (e.g., pathological lying, using only songs from the 1970s to communicate, or giving people effusive praise in order to gain social acceptance).

94

- *"Hooks"* (recurring, coined expressions).
- *Ability to work opposite of all kinds of character types.* Practice your character in situations with other strong characters. Does your character hold up?

As a curveball, your instructor could ask you to create five *new* characters at the party, based on a random suggestion. "Take the plunge" into a physical and vocal demeanor, develop a specific point of view, find a game and play it.

Summary

- *Research your character's language.* It will help you find a character game.
- *Use your prepared characters in improv,* but beware of the pitfalls.
- *Test your character range, contrast, depth, and adaptability* with Character Party.

Celebrity Impersonations

Celebrity impersonations add socio-political zing to sketch shows like *SNL* and *MadTV*. Here are some basic techniques for developing celebrity impersonations.

First, stack the deck in your favor.

- *Stick with the most recognizable figures with strong attributes.* Certain celebrities are at the top of the "most recognized" list, and are likely to elicit a stronger audience response than lesser-knowns.
- *Put your own spin on celebrities* that are too often imitated, otherwise avoid them.
- *Rely on expert fellow impersonators.* Certain fellow players have a knack for impressions. Use them as your coaches and adopt their distilled mannerisms. Once Dana Carvey captured George Bush, everyone at the office could do it.
- *Write the celebrity's game into the scene.* Write the scene so that it focuses on the celebrity's most recognizable feature or game. With lesser-knowns, reiterate the celebrity's name throughout the sketch so as to remind the audience.

Second, use a distillation process. Extract the essence of the celebrity.

- *Use your selective memory* of the celebrity's outstanding attributes before you begin. Your memory is the most heightened source for the essence of a character. What you remember about the expressions, look, sound, and history of a celebrity is what the audience remembers, too.
- *Replay videotape* of the celebrity as a primary reference tool.
- *Identify the celebrity's salient game, and exaggerate it for comic effect:* height, body weight, hairstyle, clothing, vocal inflections, expressions, rhythms, vocabulary, emotions, mannerisms, attitudes, character flaws, preoccupations, behaviors, etc.
- *Choose the celebrity's most identifiable costume and hairstyle from all time.* Oprah used to wear a shoulder scarf, and although she doesn"t anymore, it is instantly recognizable as her trademark.

Third, rehearse the attributes you discovered.

- *Use a mirror* to help you imitate the character's facial expressions.
- *Use videotape* of your own performance as a way to review your accuracy. Tape yourself as you echo the character's hooks, rhythms, vocal inflection, and physicality.

Summary

- *Stack the deck in your favor;* avoid lesser-knowns, use a coach, and write the game into the scene.
- *Use a distillation process;* use your memory, use videotape, and heighten the game and costume.
- *Rehearse the attributes* you discover, using a mirror and videotape.

Chapter 17
Character Wrap-Up

By the end of your character class, you have learned to "take the plunge" into character essences in solo and group improvs. You have practiced finding character games, fleshing out your character's history and defense mechanisms. You have used prepared characters in improvised scenes, and you've improvised and honed monologues for them. You have also learned an approach to performing celebrity impersonations.

Take stock: As I finished my character class, I became aware that improv strengthened my characters and provided an engine for my monologues. Improv keeps the information flowing, and even provides an understructure for shaping scenes.

Amassing your library of funny characters will take time. Some character comedians workshop their characters over the course of their entire careers. Be patient.

Your characters and your improv skill will serve you well in long form improv.

Summary
- *Make your characters personal,* even though they may start externally.
- *Practice "taking the plunge" into characters,* physically and vocally.
- *Grow your characters* over time by developing their history, game, longevity, and psychology.
- *Practice your characters* in improv scenes to give them depth and versatility.

Section 4
Long Form Improv

"I saw long form improv and it looked easy.

*It wasn't until I got up there to do it myself that I realized that
long form can only work if all the basic and intermediate
improv skills are firmly in place."*

— Author's Journal, January 17, 2002

Chapter 18

Introduction to Long Form Improv

Once you feel comfortable improvising single scenes (short form), you're ready for several conjoined scenes (long form). Long form builds on your intermediate improv skills and allows you to use the characters you have developed along the way. Long form also provides a firm foundation for writing comedy sketches and even film.

Long form improv is a series of interdependent improvised scenes, often following a *structure* (a template) that helps players tend to the multiple story lines.

In the 1960s, comedian and improv mastermind Del Close began linking improvised scenes while working at the Committee in San Francisco. The linked scenes were random and unstructured, and Del shelved the idea. In the 1980s, Del met Charna Halpern (now the Director of the ImprovOlympic in Chicago and ImprovOlympic West in L.A.), and together they created the idea of the *Harold* — a series of linked improvised scenes using structures that allow players to build cohesive, satisfying improvised plays.

"Harold" became synonymous with a variety of long form structures that blossomed at the ImprovOlympic under the guidance of Close and Halpern. The Harold continues to evolve in improv theaters throughout the U.S. and abroad.

Harold

The basic Harold structure is comprised of games (all players), scenes (two or more players), and monologues. The Harold starts with an opening game based on a given suggestion, followed by (usually) three subsequent scenes, a second game, and a final revisiting of scenes. There are many variations to this standard structure. For a complete explanation of the Harold refer to the book *Truth in Comedy* by Charna Halpern, Del Close, and Kim "Howard" Johnson published by Meriwether Publishing, Colorado Springs, CO, 1994.

Other Long Form Styles

Long form exists in a variety of styles outside of the Harold at the ImprovOlympic. As a simple example of what long form looks like, here's a long form structure that requires nothing more than an extemporaneous monologue, spawning a free-form series of related improv scenes. This long form starts with an opening improvised monologue based on the audience suggestion "graphic artist." Then, players improvise a series of randomly generated scenes. Together, the group of scenes is known as a long form *set*.

> *Player One (Fred): I never thought I would succeed in the corporate world, but I have! My degree is in graphic design — not exactly a great degree for working at an accounting firm. I'm afraid of climbing the corporate ladder there — I fear that someone will "unmask" me. If they find out that I am really only a graphic designer, they'll fire me. Come to think of it, I sure could design a beautiful pink slip for myself on QuarkXPress.*

Scene 1: Corporate Office meeting; all players. Executives praise Fred for the lavish looking quarterly income reports. They treat the reports like art objects. They wear surgical gloves when handling them and give Fred a promotion.

Scene 2: Auction House; Sotheby's auctioneer sells Fred's two-page quarterly sales report for an unprecedented $200,000. The buyer is financial guru Warren Buffett, normally a conservative investor, now infatuated with the reports.

Scene 3: Hospital Emergency Room; doctors perform surgery without plastic gloves. (There is a local glove shortage because all Fred's reports are handled with them.) Patients become infected.

Scene 4: Attorney's Office; ambulance-chasing attorneys talk to a patient infected by doctors who didn't use surgical gloves. The attorneys try to engage the patient in a malpractice suit. The patient dies, lovingly clutching one of Fred's reports.

Scene 5: Corporate Office; Fred is promoted to chief financial officer of the accounting firm. Fred tells them that he has only a graphic design degree. They are outraged and assault him. Fred requires surgery.

Scene 6: Operating Room; Fred is now the patient on the table. The doctors know that Fred caused the glove shortage. They abuse Fred during surgery.

Scene 7: Corporate Office; Warren Buffet visits Fred after his surgery. Buffet is angry at paying so much for a now worthless report. He pummels Fred, who requires additional surgery.

Scene 8: Operating Room; during surgery, Fred fights off doctors and buffets angry shareholders.

Scene 9: Corporate Office; recovering from surgery, Fred designs his own pink slip in Quark Express. Fellow employees start a bidding war over it.

BLACKOUT

In the example above, we see a monologue at the beginning of the set and a resulting series of *freestyle* (non-prescribed) improvised scenes. The players randomly generate the subsequent scenes, building on the themes that spring forth from the monologue. Each scene builds on the next. We revisit characters and locations throughout the set.

Another Long Form Example

The most popular long form structure is called "ABC," or "Three Scenes." The director asks the audience for a suggestion. The ensemble creates three separate improvised scenes based on the given suggestion. Each of the three scenes has a different location and pair of characters. The only thing that is planned is the order of the scenes.

Round One:	Scene A1, B1, and C1
Round Two:	Scene A2, B2, and C2
Round Three:	Scene A3, B3, and C3
Round Four:	Freestyle Scenes

Each improvised scene follows the prescribed order, and expands on the themes and ideas introduced in the previous scenes. After the nine scenes, the structure is open for freestyle scenes. The director ends the half-hour set at his discretion. The ABC structure allows us to revisit characters three times, as we see how the game affects their lives.[1]

Structure vs. Freestyle

Any given Harold-style long form has a small amount of predetermined structure: the order, frequency, duration, number of players, or location of the scenes is prearranged. Players attempt to weave the multiple storylines together, in a literal or thematic way, by the end of the set.

Freestyle long form, on the other hand, has no predetermined structure and uses the *montage* device: players discover the order, frequency, duration, number of players, *and* location of the improvised scenes as they go along, based on the action as it emerges. Players continually weave multiple storylines together. Players phase out those storylines that lack momentum and expand those storylines that add focus or depth to the emerging through-line.

Whether your long form set is structured like Harold or freestyle, the options are limitless. Structured or freestyle, you'll use the same basic long form skills:

Long Form Skill # 1: Building a Logical Absurdity Inside One Scene

Long Form Skill #2: "Circling Up" (Replicating the Problem Inside One Scene)

Long Form Skill #3: Extending the Game across Multiple Scenes

Long Form Skill #4: Editing Scenes

---

[1] A detailed analysis of long form structures like the Harold can be found in the text *Truth in Comedy* by Charna Halpern, Del Close, and Kim "Howard" Johnson, Colorado Springs, CO: Meriwether Publishing Ltd., 1994.

Chapter 19

Long Form Skill #1: Building a Logical Absurdity inside One Scene

Comedy scenes are based on logic. Each piece of information builds logically onto the next, creating a logical premise that the audience can follow.

So, you must uncover information in that important first scene step by logical step. If the premise is logical, you can build it to absurd proportions — inside one scene, or throughout an entire long form set.

Avoid laying on information from outer space. You will destroy the underlying relatability of your scene. The audience won't buy it, because it looks like you're trying to be funny. Here's an example:

Laid-on information that is unfunny and confusing.
Player One: Thanks for hemming my prom dress, Aunt Carla.
Player Two: Jenny, if you're going to be the first girl to go to prom with a space alien, I don't want his family thinking we're sloppy.
("Huh?")

Logical leaps of absurd information that are funny and clear.
Player One: Thanks for hemming my prom dress, Aunt Carla. After all, there are no tailors here in Area 51.
Player Two: Jenny, if you're the first girl to go to prom with a space alien, we don't want his family thinking we're sloppy.

In the first example, the information about the alien prom date is laid on and unfunny. In the second example, the alien information is a more logical leap of absurdity considering they live

104

Tips

> Build the comedic premise of a scene step by logical step. If this is true, then this must be true. And, if that is true, then this must be true as well.
>
> If you break the train of logic, you'll derail the comedy.

in Area 51, Nevada, and is therefore believable.

Once you establish the basic logic of a single scene, you can grow the game exponentially, inside one scene or across an entire long form set.

Take stock: Long form starts with a single scene. Don't feel pressure to be funny. Use all your tools from basic improv: foundation, emotion, object work, tempo, stage picture, character, relationship, specificity, "Yes anding," and labeling. If you focus on justifying information and building a logical premise in a *single* scene, you will have built a strong foundation for an entire long form *set*.

Summary

- *Use step-by-step logic* to build absurdity.
- *Avoid information from outer space.* Start simply.
- *Long form sets start with one logical scene.* The scene will be the basis for all the scenes that follow it.

Chapter 20

Long Form Skill #2: "Circling Up" (Replicating the Problem inside One Scene)

In your beginning improv and character classes, you practiced identifying the game in the scene. (The game is a theme or pattern in the character's lives that repeats and escalates for comic effect.) Once you identify the game in the scene, do what's called *circle up* — provide continually heightened iterations of the game.

> "I get a good scene started, and then something happens and it just dries up. What am I not doing?"
> — Author's Journal, May 15, 2001

For example, if in the first scene you establish the game that a landlord is too cheap to fix the plumbing, find another instance of his parsimony — maybe the shabby electrical outlets give the tenants merciless shocks. And another — perhaps the tenants have been holding up the roof for three weeks. And another ... So, you echo the game, replicating it (circling up) in continually heightened iterations within in the same scene.

Practice circling up. It all starts with identifying a clear game in a scene (*calling it*), and then giving examples (*delivering*).

Call and Deliver

In this revelatory exercise taught to me by Ted Michaels at The Groundlings, two players start a scene, adding foundation as usual. However, as soon as the scene progresses to the point where the player can identify a game, the instructor asks a player to "call it," e.g., "We Hamptons playboys spend frivolously without an awareness of social issues!" Then, each character demonstrates

---

three or more examples of spending money frivolously, in a politically incorrect way, preferably in the present (or from history if you must). And the scene is over.

Player One: I bought this original painting of Cesar Chavez. It matches the color scheme of my tennis court nicely.

Player Two: I bought this tennis outfit for my wife; it's one of a kind. To make sure it stays one of a kind, I'm having the sweatshop employees killed.

That's it. Set up the scene, call it, stamp out iterations of the game, and you're done.

Here's how the exercise works. Start the scene in forty seconds of silence — an incredibly long time. Two players watch each other's object work, and set up the foundation logically, gracefully, gradually, leisurely, piece by piece. Who, what, and where. Only then, when the characters are established and the game becomes apparent, the instructor "pauses" the scene and asks the actor to "call it."

Calling it, as mentioned earlier, is identifying the game in simple, clear language for all players to hear. For example, "We are eternally optimistic even though we live in poverty."

From that moment on, the players demonstrate only examples of that game: "Let's make wood soup for the holidays; we'll use the last standing tree in our yard." Example after example, iteration after iteration, until it either reaches absurd proportions or the instructor ends the scene.

With practice, players can call the game in conversation during the scene: "You are always optimistic, despite your dying." That's it. That's the game. Now each character, in turn, creates instances that demonstrate or exemplify that game.

Don't fall into the trap of recounting incidents from the past. Instead, make the iterations steeped in an active now, which will give you an activity to do in the scene.

The Call and Deliver exercise emphasizes the importance of patterns. If the audience can predict what happens next, they share the experience. Laura Petrie opens the last piece of mail, even though she promised she wouldn't, she just can't help herself ... and we know something awful will happen next, as a twenty-foot raft begins self-inflating ...

Take stock: When you "circle up," you provide continually heightened iterations of the game. This repetition is what comedy audiences crave. The audience wants to identify a pattern in the characters' behavior so that they can predict what happens next.

Tips

Avoid statements that say "We're going to ... " or "We ought to ... " or "Next time, we might ... " or "Yesterday ... " Do it now. Make it so.

Repetition is the structural foundation for improv and sketch comedy. Usually patterns repeat in threes.

Offer a lifeline to the audience by establishing the game and honoring it with continually heightened examples.

Summary

- *Identify the game and call it.* Subtly notify the others in the scene that you have identified the theme.
- *"Circle up"* by providing continually heightened instances of the game.
- *Repetition seduces the audience* into predicting what happens next.

Chapter 21

Long Form Skill #3: Extending the Game across Multiple Scenes

Now that you have replicated the game in the current scene, extrapolate how the game impacts the rest of the world. If it is true that the landlord is cheap, what else is true? Maybe he lets cows graze on the front lawn rather than mow it. We know that the broken electrical outlets give shocks and the tenants have been holding up the roof. Maybe the tenants have become quite muscular. Perhaps they have become bodybuilders who are afraid of electricity.

Allow the various games in the scene to influence other people and places in that fictional world. If this is true for these people, then this must be true as well. And if that is true, this must be true as well.

Tips

> In long form, mirror the previous scenes and heighten the existing themes.
>
> In long form, when in doubt, be a relative. Be someone with high-stakes ties to the main character, and who is close to them.

In freestyle sections, you can create new scenes from the fun secondary references in other scenes. For example, if a character in the first scene mentions that the government is using inefficient methods to promote the new tax policy, create a scene with government skywriters in an airplane having difficulty skywriting the words "fiscal accountability." Also, if the characters you introduce are memorable, bring them back for another scene where their predicament has heightened or changed based on the new information that has emerged.

If another character adopts an absurd, uncomfortable, or even a politically incorrect characteristic, like "homophobic," give yourself that characteristic, too. Ugly as it is, make it endemic in this fictional cohesive world. Spread homophobia, and thereby lampoon its absurdity. To deny a politically incorrect action by backing away from it is to deny your fellow player. You endanger the continuity of the long form, which thrives on cohesive, justified absurdities.

Types of Scenes

Each scene in a long form reflects the concepts and themes established in the previous scenes. When you initiate new scenes, use these guidelines:

- *Revisit a previously established scene or character.* Start the same scene earlier or later in time, advancing the scene based on new information. (If the United Nations has its annual meeting in a French fishing village, later we may see the counsel members transfixed with comparing fishing lure hats, disrupting their session.) Or start a new scene using an established character in a new, related predicament. (The UN representative from Chad mandates fishing in his own country, even though it's landlocked.)
- *Create a parallel scene.* Introduce new characters in a similar predicament, furthering an established game. (If it worked for Chad, now Western Australia is trying it.)
- *Create a tangential scene.* Introduce new characters based on secondary information in the previous scene. (If the UN's floral arrangements are deemed ugly in the first scene, maybe we see a second scene where defiant gardeners grow fields full of hideous flowers on purpose, as an antiestablishment message.)
- *Add a scene based on an improviser's error.* Justify and support a player's mistake or any incongruent information. (If a player misidentifies Chad as being in Europe, later we may see a scene where safari animals run free through Trafalgar Square.)

Building Accord, Not Accuracy

Don't make your scene *accurate* in "normal world" terms. Instead build *accord* between your absurd scenes. In other words, don't introduce scenes with people who don't understand the absurdity or who reject it in real world terms. (Avoid "These town folk are crazy! They're all wearing chicken suits for the media!") *Instead, introduce characters who adopt the absurdity according to its inherent logic, extend it and expand it.* ("I may only be a small town reverend, but this town's chicken processing plant is our only hope for fame! God forgive me, I'm wearing a chicken suit, too! Now, let's start this church service ... ")

In long form, and in all improv, know everything about everyone and everything that has happened everywhere. Don't pretend not to know information about other characters and scenes. This bogs down the action. Know it all, extend the game, and heighten it.

With the following exercise, create a single scene that builds a world of *cohesive* absurdity. Don't force the scene to *correspond* to the normal world.

Tips

Avoid letting the game of the long form take over, precluding established characters. Remember to bring back established characters, even as the set peaks.

If your character would probably say "no," but the improv rule is to say "yes," do so reluctantly, or at a price: "Okay, I'll do it. Normally I wouldn't kill anyone, but I'll have to if I'm ever to play with the Chicago Symphony."

Godot

This extraordinary exercise was developed by Stan Wells of the Empty Stage and has since migrated to The Groundlings. The exercise takes away your routine of adding foundation: who, what, and where. Instead, you must focus on a simple, sparse conversation, which sets up a game between the two characters in a single scene.

As in *Waiting for Godot* by Samuel Beckett, nothing happens in this exercise except moments between two people. Don't do object work. Don't even add foundation, or at least add very little. Use sparse dialogue. There are no additional scenes. There is only a box and a chair available to the players, like the rock and tree in Godot. Put your body in a strong, evocative position to create a lively stage picture to start the scene. Use the silence to observe one another. Do not refer to the outside world, just these people in this room, talking to one another. The players must find a game in the minutiae of their relationship without using the usual trappings of object work and lots of dialogue. The scene should have a pithy, abstract quality. The players must be intensely focused on finding a game from the smallest detail. This exercise ends up being a test to see if players can connect with each other to find a simple pattern to their relationship.

For example, one character worships the other who won't reciprocate. That's it. That's the game. Replicate it. Players need very little to build a solid premise. These scenes have the feel of familiar comedy sketches — very little dialogue and just the sparsest comedic structure. The scenes are often absurd, but they make sense on a gut level. For example, a woman has a box stuck to her abdomen, and her lover tells her he's going to leave her because of her "problem."

The least successful scenes are ones that are too complex. Instead, stick to a simple game and replicate the action. This exercise proves that there's no need to create a grand narrative plot, even if you're doing a long form set. Simpler is better. Trust that you can find a simple game from very little in the first few lines of your improv.

Now that you have extended a game across multiple scenes, you are ready to practice editing the scenes together.

Take stock: Long form requires all the basic scene skills, character skills, game skills, and building a cohesive world of absurdity. Keep all the plates spinning at once.

> ### *Tip*
> *Use an unusual part of the stage during improv to create a scene based on a unique stage picture: the floor, the walls, windows, the edge of the stage, and even the audience.*

112

Summary

- *Initiate new scenes based on previous scenes.* New scenes can be a revisiting of a previous scene, parallel scenes, tangential scenes, or scenes justifying an error.
- *Build a world of accord, not accuracy.* The fictitious world should contain its own intrinsic law, not real-world legality.
- *Allow the game to affect other parts of this world.* Extend the game, and heighten the themes in other scenes.

Chapter 22

Long Form Skill #4: Editing Scenes

So far, you have concentrated on building a logical absurdity, circling up, and extending the game across multiple scenes. Now focus on the skill of editing.

In long form, all players stand upstage, or just offstage, ready to join the action, down center. Usually there are two chairs upstage, which players retrieve as needed and return when the scene ends.

Usually, long form scenes begin and end at the discretion of the players. (Players sense when a previous scene has reached its peak.) Two or more players *edit* (cut off) the current scene and replace it by initiating their own new scene. There are many methods for editing scenes in long form. The most popular methods are listed below:

- *Tapping* one of the current players on the shoulder
- *Walking in front* of the current players
- *"Clapping in,"* where players clap their hands to notify the players you are ending their scene and initiating another. (This method works best with freestyle montage sets, like the ones performed by the Empty Stage.)

The director calls a *blackout* (cutting off the lights) at the appropriate time, usually at the peak of the freestyle scenes, or when the set has run its course. The director uses his judgment to determine the exact moment of blackout — when there is a sense of closure, resolution, or denoument.

> **Tip**
>
> In long form, as the current players exit, they may trail off with a quick closing line to help fill in the pause as the new players replace them.

In each three-hour class, you'll likely start with warmup exercises specific to long form improv. Then you'll perform a few long form sets of varying lengths, from fifteen minutes to an hour each. The following is a sample long form. Use it as an exercise in class or in performance. Use all the improv skills you have amassed — from building the foundation, to adding characters, growing the game,

Long Form — Famous Artist

Group. The instructor designates one player to be a popular painter or sculptor, e.g., Picasso. Start a biographical two-person scene loosely based on the painter's life, with some discussion beforehand about where he lives or his current predicament. The players aren't doing a realistic re-creation of the painter's life, but rather, a heightened version of the painter in a world of his own logic. Initiate new freestyle scenes based on the information revealed in the previous scenes. During this long form, the painter can monologize while he paints, narrating future action. Also, two other players can be the stylized (disjointed, blurred, blue) painted versions of himself as he appears in his work. The instructor directs the first scenes. Later, all players are allowed to initiate any scene, old or new. The focus in this exercise is extending the game; initiating new scenes based on previous scenes; building a world of accord, not accuracy; allowing the game to affect other parts of this world.

extending themes, and editing.

Take stock: As you try your hand at long form, remember your sense of group mind. Work in tandem with your fellow players to create a flow of scenes around the central theme. The more you work with your fellow players, the more intuitive the process of editing and initiating scenes becomes.

Summary
- *Edit and initiate new scenes* using any agreed upon method. "Tapping in," walking in front of, and "clapping In."
- *Practice creating long form around one character.* The lead character can provide the backbone for a series of freestyle scenes.

Chapter 23

Long Form Extras

Exercises

Long Form Preparation Exercises

The exercises titled Long Form Preparation Exercises in the appendix on page 178 emphasize "Yes anding," listening, circling up, confirming and extending absurd information, and building cohesive absurdity. All these skills are essential for building long form improv.

Long Form Structures

The exercises called Long Form Structures in the appendix on page 180 are great for performance. They are freestyle long form structures, allowing players to create scenes and revisit them at random, without the burden of a prescribed scene order.

Long Form — Don't Plan Ahead

Don't plan long-term plots in long form improv. Keep it simple. Avoid "I can't wait to race this car at the track tomorrow night," because the scene gets bogged down waiting for a future event. Also, we're obliged to show that future event — there's no surprise or spontaneity. Instead, say "I assume my Chevy Malibu runs okay; I'm more concerned about the way it looks." This leaves your scene options open. Later, we may see a scene where the town is so obsessed with the look of its antique cars that even the government's vintage ambulances must be pushed to their destinations. We may never get to the racetrack.

> ### Tips
>
> In long form improv, label characters in other related scenes by describing a problem they're having or by describing their physical traits. Give them something to play.
>
> Even in long form, remember the basic ways to add information: dialogue, object work, stage picture, character, emotion, and tempo.

Cheating

As you begin to practice long form sets in class, the instructor *cheats* by guiding the progression of scenes. For example, the instructor may guide the opening of the long form set by selecting characters or situations for the opening scenes, and whisper suggestions for subsequent scene ideas. As the students become more adept at shaping open long form sets, the instructor steps back to allow the players free reign.

Another helpful "cheat" for beginners is to communicate the scene idea to fellow players in a whisper just before the scene starts. This allows the initiating player to communicate the who, what, or where in the scene in a few brief words. Also, players can openly beckon to other players as they enter for the scene edit, to assemble the players quickly. Later, this assembly process becomes silent as players develop a group mind.

Bartender, Don't Cut Me Off

As players grow confident, they have more and more ideas for initiating scenes. Sometimes, however, players

Tips

Don't add such weird information that the scene becomes implausible or the character becomes crazy. Make your information quirky, offbeat, and even strange, but within the cohesive logic and reason of the scene.

Establish and repeat character names during an improv, helping to remind all the players. This makes it easier to call back characters into new scenes.

Initiating players must set up the foundation of a scene immediately with who, what, and where. (In the middle of a complicated set with multiple storylines, players must continually re-orient each other.)

Avoid initiating a scene that is only a one-joke gag. (If your fellow players don't initiate a replacement scene, you're stuck in your one-joke scene for longer than you thought.)

become drunk with power. They edit and replace the current scene before it has a chance to mature. Listen to the current scene and ask yourself the following questions about the current scene *before* you initiate:

- Are the players struggling, or are the players confidently advancing an established game?
- Are these established characters, or new characters that

require more time?
- Is the scene a one-gag idea that requires an immediate edit?
- Has the scene idea run its course?

Develop an awareness of the needs of the current scene and edit it at its peak.

Create Your Own Long Form Structures

Improv theaters continually create new long form structures. Structures often rely on time-honored comedy devices. Some devices are listed here:

- *Playing with time* (flashforwards, flashbacks, historical contexts, time travel, juxtaposed generations, condensed time, back and forth between two time periods)
- *Playing with locations* (opposite locations experiencing the same problem, e.g., heaven and hell; "split screen," where two scenes happen simultaneously as one player peforms in both scenes; "fish out of water" locations where characters are struggling with the lay of the land)
- *Playing with character* (central character changes over time; central character contaminates his whole community with the same point of view; character changes jobs, bringing his old habits with him; character experiences emotional changes)

Themes

Any social phenomenon can become a launching point for a long form improv. The best "seed" suggestions for starting a long form improv are those that allow the players room to grow. Avoid suggestions that are too literal or tied inextricably to a real-world scenario. Avoid depressing themes and blue humor. The following are some "seed" suggestions for long form themes.

- **Newspaper Headlines of the Day** ("First Manned Balloon Around the World" and "Enron Executives Testify")
- **Coming of Age** (Create a not-so-typical teen story, filled with angst about relationships, a mentor, contentious parents, and the girl next door.)

- **TV Phenomena** (Create made-up episodes of classic shows as they "jump the shark.")
- **Fiction Styles** (Jack Kerouac, Ray Bradbury, William Conrad, or Raymond Chandler)
- **Technology Phenomena** (Instant messaging at the Knights of the Round Table; using PDAs on deserted islands; web logs [blogs] of the rich and famous)
- **Players' Personal Stories** (Real testimonials around a theme like "Language Barriers" or "UFO Sightings")
- **Pop Psychology** (Rural communities live and die by pop psychology principles; modern psychiatrists run for political office)
- **Philosophy** (Ancient philosophers with character flaws; ancient philosophers and religious figures transplanted into modern times)

Long Form's Influence on Sketch Comedy

Although transforming long form improv into plays, TV series, and films is relatively new territory, The Second City broke new ground in live performance with *Piñata Full of Bees,* where they linked written sketch comedy scenes in a satisfying and cohesive long form theater style. *The Upright Citizens Brigade* on Comedy Central succeeded in transforming long form structure to a half hour format for TV. *Mr. Show* on HBO used a long form technique to loosely link their various sketches.

Although long form improv has been around for a couple of decades, long form sketch comedy as adapted for TV and film is in the nascent stages.

Take stock: Long form opens your mind to new understructures for screenwriting. Improvised long form breaks the mold of the "Act I, II, III" screenwriting formula. It gets your brain working on writing pieces that last longer than three to four minutes. It encourages you to think in new ways about the transitions, narrative, plot, and theme. Long form allows comedians, actors, and writers to think beyond the three-minute medium as they exercise their improv skills.

Summary

- *Don't plan ahead.* Leave your scene options open so you can discover new scenes in the moment.
- *You're allowed to cheat* while you learn long form. Whisper to your scene partners and accept suggestions from the instructor.
- *Don't be overzealous in editing;* give scenes the time they require.
- *Create your own long form structures* using time, location, and characters.

Chapter 24

Long Form Wrap-Up

Take stock: The lessons you learn in long form will strengthen your writing skill. Using logic, developing and calling the game, and heightening the premise are primary tools for writing original sketches in your next class.

Summary
- *Use step-by-step logic* to build absurdity — in one scene or across many.
- *Call the game*, circle up, and extend the themes.
- *Try both Harold and freestyle* long form to see which suits you.
- *Create your own long form structures.* Use long form to spur you on to write short films, feature-length films, and plays.

Section 5
Writing Sketch Comedy

"At the end of my first writing class, we performed our sketch show. When the audience laughed at the sketches I wrote, I thought I was going to cry.

All the character exploration, the structuring, the re-writes, the timing, the haggling with fellow writers, and all the sketch material that wound up on the cutting room floor — it's so much work.

This stuff is so much harder than it looks. I didn't know until I did it.

Now when an audience member capriciously ridicules a sketch, I want to flog them."

— Author's Journal, February 28, 2002

Chapter 25

Sketches: Getting Started

The good news is that if you can improvise a scene, you can write one. All the rules of improvising apply to writing, and improv is a great way to develop sketch material. Review the Comedy Commandments in Section 2, and recognize that *you've already honed your writing technique through improv:*

- **Foundation — Who, What, and Where.** (Written scenes need efficient exposition, too.)
- **Six types of information:** Object work, tempo, emotions, character, stage picture, and dialogue. (Sketches require these components just like improv. Any one component can be the focus of a written sketch; more than two missing components may weaken your sketch.)
- **Start in the *middle* of the scene.** (Avoid writing about the status quo; get right to the high-stakes, emotional action.)
- **Don't negate or deny.** (In a blind sketch from scratch, negation and denial confuse the audience and slow down the action.)
- **Don't argue.** (Limit tedious, lengthy arguments in sketches.)
- **Don't instruct or teach.** (Avoid the plodding pace of a teaching scenario in your written sketches, too.)
- **Don't ask questions. Endow.** (Advance your sketch with efficient statements, not expository questions.)
- **Avoid playing crazy.** (Wildly irrational characters without any consistency make it hard to write a game into short scenes.)
- **Don't plan ahead.** (Don't try to write a complicated plot. It's only a three-minute medium. Keep it simple.)
- **Don't do blue humor. Don't be recklessly offensive.** (Keep your sketches out of the gutter. Remember, if you write a foul sketch, you may be stuck performing it for *weeks*.)
- **Don't make jokes.** Engage your sketch characters in a

dramatic action, not just a verbal volley of one-liners and quips.)

- **Don't play strangers.** (Sketch setups are more efficient and heightened when the characters know one another.)
- **"Yes and."** (Sketch characters must agree, justify, explore, and heighten the game. Avoid *"Just go away!"* sketches.)
- **Give and take.** (Be generous. Don't favor your own character to the exclusion of the other players in the scene. Balance your writing.)
- **Work together.** (When you write alone, you'll need feedback more than ever.)

Despite your improv advantage, when you begin to write sketch comedy, you'll meet with some hard lessons, like I did: how to hone dialogue, how to build sketch structure, and how to collaborate with just about anyone.

> *"What's the point of forcing us to write together?*
> *It's not like this in the real world ... Is it?"*
> — Author's Journal, November 2, 2001

The Classes

Sketch writing classes are hands on — you write and perform monologues, sketches, and improv for a public performance at the end of a six-, eight-, or twelve-week class. The instructor is usually a professional comedy writer and performer, and is usually a veteran company member. Like the other

> *There is no manual, no syllabus or handouts. Keep a class journal, recording the exercises and instructor feedback.*

comedy classes, there is no manual, and the learning is experiential. You improvise a scene with a partner, transcribe the scene, perform it, learn from your mistakes, and receive instructor feedback as you go.

You work in a state of "forced collaboration": you must commit to writing with your randomly selected partners and commit to transforming your improvised scenes into workable written premises.

Usually writing classes include a performance, where students perform the material that they have written for themselves. This makes the class doubly intense, burdening performers with a large number of writing assignments and characters to create in six or twelve weeks.

Most writing classes begin with an intimate student introduction in a circle. The group must begin to act as a tight-knit ensemble in order to present material in a public performance at the end of the class.

The following chapters will strengthen your sketch writing skills and help you prepare for sketch show performances:

- Finding and Shaping Sketch Material
- The Sketch Writing Toolbox
- Getting Your Sketch on Its Feet

Tips

Heed your instructor's feedback. Each instructor note has layers of meaning beyond its initial application. Learn from others' mistakes.

Type your scenes in standard script format, including the writers' names, version number, and date.

Chapter 26
Finding and Shaping Sketch Material

Comedy writing is a fast-paced business. Sometimes sitcom writers crank out an episode in one week or less. Often, writers are on the live set, rewriting lines as the cameras roll. Just like improv, they're handed a given premise and they run with it. Comedy writers can't cling to sketches that they wrote a year ago. They must continually harness their natural flow of comic observations, and make a daily habit of translating those observations into written form. The same holds true for you in your comedy writing class.

Turning Life into Sketch Comedy

Some students nervously stockpile sketches in advance of a writing class, fearing that they will run out of honed material and fail.

The problem isn't the lack of sketch ideas. The challenge is to develop the writing muscle to harness your *everyday* comic observations into structured written material.

Starting with an Observation

Start simply. Observe a social or behavioral phenomenon, and jot it down in a handy notebook, e.g., "I've noticed how most L.A. copy store employees are really out-of-work filmmakers. They know about film, but they know nothing about copy machines."

Practice identifying those moments during your day when you say to yourself, "That is so pathetic! Outrageous! Absurd!" Then, jot it down. For example, today on an airplane, I saw a grown woman in a business suit suck her thumb because she was frightened of flying. She tried to hide it behind one of those cheap pillows the airlines give you. "Outrageous!" (Jot.) I also noticed that CNN has an airport version of their news program, completely censored of any news about airline bankruptcies. "Pathetic!" (Jot.)

As long as you have a strong opinion about it, any social or behavioral phenomenon can be a jumping-off point for a character or sketch: any observed human behavior, an odd locale, an expression, a color, a word, an emotion, or even a strange chemical element like Boron. Even if an idea is someone else's, use the power of improv to develop a strong point of view and create the premise.

Improvising, Transcribing, and Rearranging

Using your observation as the topic, improvise the scene with a partner. Be sure to add the foundation: who, what, and where. Allow the improv to find its own game — it may be different than the one you planned. After the improv, transcribe the dialogue and action in script form, even if you aren't satisfied with it.

Looking at your transcribed improv, create an outline of the action. Define what happens in each beat. Then, rearrange and *heighten* the action. Rearrange the instances of the game so that each instance builds on the one before it. Heighten the game by adding new actions that you may not have thought of during the improv.

Staying with our L.A. copy store observation, here's a sample sequence of events. (Some of the bits were from the improv, some of the bits were created *after* the improv.)

Bit 1: *Screenwriter enters a copy store to get his script copies. Copy guy is a leech who reveals he's a screenwriter too.*

Bit 2: *Screenwriter again asks for his script copies. Copy guy reveals he read the script and recommends changes.*

Bit 3: *The angry screenwriter demands the copies. The copy guy boldly reveals he already edited the screenwriter's script.*

Blow: *The livid screenwriter grabs his script copies. The copy guy tells him he changed the lead character name to his own. Now, the screenwriter owes him royalties.*

Blackout

Structuring the Action Sequence with "The Rule of Three"

You'll notice that almost all sketches have three recurring instances of the established game. Why three? It takes two instances to establish a pattern and a third to confirm it. Four instances is just blind repetition. (However, it is customary to use a heightened fourth instance as an unexpected final blow to end a sketch.)

So far, you've structured a simple scene outline based on an observation, improvised the premise, and rearranged three recurring examples of the game with a heightened final example (blow) for an ending. Later, this outline will be called a "storyboard."

Translating Observations into an Action Sequence

For further practice, look at these social observations and imagine a sequence of events from them:

• Acid rock band members are tough onstage, but turn into wimps at the sight of real blood.

• Stage mothers try to horn in on their children's fame.

• Costco employees can barely lift the huge products they sell.

• Tour guides say their speech so many times it sounds like gibberish, which annoys the tourists.

Explore and heighten each of these ideas. Imagine the action sequence for each scene, and jot it down.

The Revision Cycle

Once you improvise a scene, sit down at a computer or typewriter and capture what works: character, dialogue, action, relationship, and movement. If it's a two-person scene, re-join your partner, compare scripts, and get the sketch on its feet. (If it's a monologue, do the prep work alone.) Perform the scene and receive feedback from the instructor and your classmates. Revise and hone the sketch, exploring and heightening the parts that work, and rending the parts that don't. Repeat the revision cycle until you have a workable script.

Characters from Adjective and Occupation — Monologue
This monologue exercise is based on an assigned attribute and occupation like "Defensive Blood Doctor." You improvise the monologue and transcribe it into written form.

Create a character with a distinct point of view, create the foundation for the scene (who, what, and where), and then improvise it for instructor critique.

Based on the given adjective and occupation, here's what I improvised in class:

> **Dr. Heller:** *Mr. Fatima, your diabetes medicine was sitting on our pharmacy counter. I'm sorry I waited a week to give you back your medicine. I hope it isn't a problem, but we have been without an assistant for the job. We don't know why no one is applying.*
>
> *Let this in no way reflect the quality of this doctor, or Our Lady of Legal Mercy Hospital, where the patient is usually king, and I want to cover myself by saying "usually," so that there will be no lawsuits. We have three pending suits, and we're hurting badly. If you have a recommendation for an attorney, we would not mind getting that from you...*

Here are the instructor's comments on the performance.

Instructor's Feedback
• Make him smart, but flowing. Less rigid.
• Give him an answer for everything. That's his game.
• Make him more natural — slightly more human so we buy it.
• Rewrite it and present it for the next class.

Example of a Monologue Final Draft

I incorporated the instructor's feedback and rewrote the monologue at home, specifying the character to whom I was talking. I also added a hook, and raised the stakes by making the patient pass out in front of me. Here's the revised, edited monologue:

INT. OUR LADY OF LEGAL MERCY HOSPITAL FOYER

Dr. Mitch Heller talks with an irate patient, Julio Fatima.

DR. HELLER: (Cold and bureaucratic) *Mr. Fatima, our nurses found your diabetes medicine hidden under a stack of malpractice correspondence. We are deeply, deeply, deeply sorry.*

The nurses confused your medicine with evidence in one of the many legal cases against us and misfiled it. Our poor nurses work all day in surgery and study malpractice law at night, and they are exhausted.

On behalf of all of the doctors, including me, at Our Lady of Legal Mercy Hospital, we apologize for this one-time snafu, et cetera, et cetera, and our motto remains, "We Care ... Asterisk."

No, your recent coma was completely unrelated to your misplaced medicine, footnote one; and we are in no way responsible for your subsequent loss of limb, footnote two, ibid.

Yes, I am a doctor. But due to my heavy legal caseload, I cannot test your blood sugar right now. Please reserve a time on my new online diary and docket at Our Lady of Legal Mercy jurisprudence dot org, all one word, lower case, no spaces.

Regarding your complaint about my cold bedside manner ... I love my patients, and I want to make sure all their illnesses are settled amicably.

Mr. Fatima, don't faint in the common areas of the hospital, your insurance does not cover it, talis qualis. If you get up and move to the emergency room, we may be able to administer lifesaving support, pending review.

To help guide you to the emergency room, I've printed a map of the hospital, it's copyrighted, and here's a compass. Because we care, both items are free ... asterisk.

131

Uberrima fides, we removed your car from our parking structure and sold it to pay your overdue life insurance, and changed the beneficiary to ... us.

You're looking peaked, Mr. Fatima. If you need a transcript and table of authorities of this conversation, they are available to you in our post-op courtroom.

Carpe diem, Mr. Fatima, and I sincerely hope you get out of here alive ... asterisk.

Blackout

Take stock: Exercises like these are hit and miss. Take the pressure off yourself by enjoying improvising a character and his game. You have plenty of time to rewrite and hone the dialogue after the initial performance.

In writing class, never ditch the improvised scene, even though you may want to. Stick with it. A primary objective of any writing class is to parallel professional writing assignments. You must figure out how to fix the scene, even when you may not want to.

> ## *Tips*
>
> *As in improv, your monologue's first line should contain foundational elements, but without being too obvious or expository.*
>
> *The opening lines subtly set up the foundation and encapsulate the game. The audience should relate instantly and have expectations about what happens next.*

Exercises

Exercises for Writing Character Monologues
The exercises detailed in the appendix on page 182 will help you develop character monologues for sketch shows.

Great Character Improvs for Use in Sketch Shows
The exercises in the appendix on page 182 are character improvs that can add variety to your sketch show. These improvs impress audiences, because you develop characters instantaneously, based on audience suggestions.

Sketch Exercises — Get Your Sketch Material Here
A variety of exercises appear in the appendix on page 184.

These exercises will help you develop sketches that have historical, character-based, or physical premises.

Take stock: When you're in the middle of writing or revising a scene, it's hard to know why it's not working. Why aren't fellow players laughing? Is it the character? Is it the dialogue? Is the game unclear? To help you troubleshoot, start by reviewing the same guidelines that you use to fix an improv.

Guidelines

Monologue Guidelines

After you've written your monologue, see what's missing by reviewing this checklist:

- *Foundation.* Who, what, and where. Who is your character talking to? Don't forget the foundation — it solidifies the premise.
- *High stakes.* Make the scene important to your character. It's the big day. Sometimes you're so busy developing the character, you forget to raise the stakes in the scene.
- *A universally human character flaw.* Build a character game. Sometimes you're so focused on the clever predicament or incident in the scene that the character's flaw gets short shrift.
- *Unique physical and vocal expressions.* How is the character different than you?
- *A clear structure.* Don't let the sketch wander. Use a pattern of recurring *beats* (units of action).
- *Well-drawn characters can survive outside this scene,* without the aid of the scene's predicament. Don't make your character solely dependent on a single location or incident.

Tips

In group improvs, don't play the same character attributes as everyone else. Give yourself a different status (rank) or type. If you're all priests, make yourself a bishop. If you're all bishops, make yourself Benedictine.

Avoid pulling a gun in a scene — it forces control over your partner. Don't control or command.

Never die in a scene — stay alive. Or become a ghost. (Dying is like abandoning the scene.) Also, don't tell anyone to "get out of here." They will, and then you're stuck improvising alone.

Sketch Guidelines

After you've written your sketch, see what's missing by reviewing this checklist:

- *Heightened central characters* with a strong objective. An incident, location, or predicament is not enough.
- *A game* — a recognizable ironic pattern of dialogue or action. Without structure, the scene wanders.
- *Social or behavioral commentary,* current event reference, parody, or impersonations. Give the scene some social or behavioral significance.
- *Specific, unique information* on the topic. Specifics heighten the scene and help you avoid the cliché.
- *Unique physical action,* music, song or dance, use of stage area, props, costumes, or special effects. Avoid "talking head" sketches without an activity.

Tips

> Sketches with music, song, dance, or special skills are more likely to be selected for performance because they add variety to the standard lineup of "talking head" sketches.
>
> The opening stage picture should encapsulate the scene and set it up. The audience should get a sense of what is about to happen.

Summary

- *Use your life observations* as your wellspring of comedy material.
- *Transcribe your improvs* as a way to build a sketch quickly.
- *Structure an action sequence* based on the scene's game.
- *Learn the basic sketch and monologue guidelines;* use the checklist as a troubleshooting guide.

Chapter 27
The Sketch Writing Toolbox

Once you finish transcribing your improv, you'll have material in hand — either a three- to four-page typewritten sketch or a one- to two-page monologue. You and your writing partner will perform the sketch for your fellow players or read it to them aloud. Suddenly you may find that your great ideas are now lifeless. Players stumble over your dialogue, ruining the timing. Lines that you thought would get big laughs are met with confused silence. Players' improvised lines get bigger laughs than what you wrote, and everyone has a hundred suggestions for changing it. Welcome to the jungle.

The following sections will help you polish and structure your sketches:
- Revising — Sketch Comedy Shorthand
- The Understructure of Sketchwriting

Revising — Sketch Comedy Shorthand

It's an advanced skill to troubleshoot a sketch you've written — there are so many variables. The best way to troubleshoot a sketch is to use a surgical approach — target the problem and leave the funny part intact.

Instructors and directors use the following coined side-coaching phrases as a surgical approach to quick-fix an ailing sketch. Use these expressions when you give feedback to your fellow players. You'll be less threatening, and your partners are more likely to comply because you're using standardized comedy shorthand.

Troubleshooting Sketch and Monologue Content
- *I think you've got two sketches here.* Beware of overloading sketches with too many points of focus. Split an overloaded sketch into two separate scenes, and hone them individually.

- *Avoid inside jokes.* Would this sketch work if we don't know you personally? The audience doesn't know you and won't get the inside joke.
- *Avoid blind alleys.* Sometimes the scene setup ends up taking over the sketch. Keep your setups brief.
- *Raise the stakes.* Try changing the "where" to one that is opposite the character's normal nature. Make this the big day.
- *Set up the game immediately,* in the first few lines of the sketch, so we can "ride with you."
- *Political satire must entertain two audiences:* those who get the high concept, and those who don't.
- *I don't buy it.* Do we believe the logic in this scene? The absurd information? If we don't believe it, the comedy will appear contrived.
- *Why are we doing this sketch?* What's the concept behind it? Is it worth the effort? Bring out the social relevance.
- *Heighten it!* Make sure each instance of the game is stronger than the previous instance.

Troubleshooting Character

- *Charisma or horrisma?* ("Horrisma" is a term coined by Groundling Steve Hibbert.) We should know in the first beat whether the lead character is the protagonist or antagonist. Do we *love* him, or *love to hate* him? Is he one of *us,* or one of *them?*
- *Avoid the cliché.* Find something original about this character to separate him from the "old joke."
- *Add visual interest to a character* by laying an observed physical trait or mannerism.
- *Develop a hook,* which is a repeating character expression or behavior.

Troubleshooting Dialogue

- *Don't talk about the past.* Instead, show the past through the current action.
- *Brevity is the soul of wit.* Shorten everything.
- *Be specific with the information in a scene.* Don't use vague pronouns like "my friends" or "something." Instead, use the

character's lingo ("my hoodies"), and specific brand name pronouns (Phenphen).

- ***Don't talk about it; do it.*** Get right to the action without delay.

"It's easy for me to rely on the instructor to fix my sketch. It's harder to learn to troubleshoot scenes myself, but I'm better off in the long run."
— *Author's Journal, November 2, 2001*

Take stock: When you receive a suggestion for change, consider the source. What is the expertise of the critic? Are they using constructive, standardized feedback? Do they offer replacement suggestions or only criticism? Try implementing the suggested changes and get the sketch on its feet again, as part of the writing cycle. Retain the revisions that work and delete the revisions that don't.

> ## *Tips*
>
> *If you find a good character in a scene that didn't work, keep that character in mind for a future scene.*
>
> *Some instructors don't formally address improv theory or writing technique. The learning is in the doing. Some instructors rely on brief "sound byte" coaching phrases only.*

The Understructure of Sketch Writing

At this point, you have probably tried your hand at writing sketches using some of the improv exercises listed in the appendix, or from an idea of your own. You may have experienced the "Page Two Blues," where your idea fizzles after the first page. You may have experienced the "Can't Find an Ending to Save My Life" virus. You may have experienced the "Here's a Suggestion" syndrome, where a deluge of critics send your sketch into a tailspin. This is a great place to be, believe it or not. You are at a point where you want to know about sketch structure.

Repetition

We learned that improvised scenes use *repetition* — a pattern of actions or expressions that establish a game. Sketches contain repetition, too. Recurring internal beats lend structure and irony to sketches. Repetition allows the audience to predict what happens next. If there's no repetition, the audience asks, "Where is this going?" and "What is the point of this scene?". You can tell when the audience is confused, because they're quiet.

> *"I don't worry about structure in my sketches.*
> *My premises aren't formulaic. They're abstract.*
> *(I do have trouble finding an ending, though.)"*
> — Author's Journal, November 3, 2001

Here are some examples of classic comedy sketches with a clear use of repetition.

This *I Love Lucy* segment featuring Lucille Ball is a classic game of one-upsmanship, set in an Italian vineyard:

1. *Lucy imitates Italian woman stomping grapes. Woman stomps harder.*
2. *Lucy imitates woman. Woman stomps even harder, with more flare.*
3. *Lucy imitates woman. Blatant competition ensues.*
4. *BLOW: Woman tackles Lucy. They brawl.*

Here's another example of repetition. This *SNL* sketch, "Racist Word Association Interview," features Chevy Chase and Richard Pryor:

1. *Chase offers words; Pryor answers normally.*
2. *Offensive words; Pryor answers defensively.*
3. *Racist words; Pryor threatens back with racist words.*
4. *BLOW: Chase says, "You're hired, take two weeks off."*

The Game

You have built a game (a comic theme or gist) into improvised scenes and characters. Now build a game into your sketches. Set up the game at the beginning of the scene so the audience can "ride with you." You must state the game clearly and immediately — show the audience the game in the first few lines of dialogue. The game in Monty Python's famous "Parrot Sketch" is set up in the first line:

Customer: *Hello, I wish to register a complaint.*

(The owner does not respond.)

138

The first few lines of a sketch are like Haiku poetry. Nothing extraneous is allowed. The audience is searching for the pattern — they want to "get" it. So, the longer you wait to show the audience the game, the more confused and impatient they become.

Here's another sample game:

> **Player One:** *I'm here to pick up my script copies, under the name "Allen."*
>
> **Player Two:** *Yeah ... there was a little problem with your script. The third act was way too long, so I cut it.*

The first beat should contain the first instance of the game — a copy attendant oversteps his boundaries and edits a customer's screenplay. Immediately address the audience's question "What am I supposed to *get* here?" Answer them in the first few lines. Good sketches build an underlying "trust" with the audience. If you switch the game mid-sketch, give them a blind alley, or wait until page two to show them the game, the audience will have given up on you.

Comedy Structures

Once I had some sketch writing under my belt, I was able to identify familiar comedy structures that I see in theater, TV, and film. By developing a list of comedy structures, I can categorize types of comedy based the situation, action, or point of focus. When I have a context for the type of sketch I'm writing, I have examples to draw from, making it easier to shape the structure of the sketch and find an ending. These structures even apply to writing comedic advertising copy

Tips

Avoid blind alleys — usually an introductory segment used to set up a scene becomes a mini-scene in itself, leading nowhere and bogging down the scene. Setups must be quick and efficient.

Even in sketches, avoid arguments. Instead, identify an incongruity in the characters' lives and show how the characters work together against that problem.

Don't fix the other character's problem; pour gasoline on it. "Sorry, doctor, these dirty scalpels are all I have. Hachooo!"

As you watch comedy, try to identify the comic structure that the writers are using in any given scene.

— from TV commercials to billboards. The following is a partial list of structures, along with current examples. (Some of the structures listed below also work as performance improvs.)

Structure	*Examples*
Fish Out of Water This structure features a character who can't adapt to a new environment—either a strange man in a normal land or a normal man in a strange land. (This all-encompassing structure applies to *any* sketch — a character, activity, location, visual element, or emotion that doesn't belong in its current context.)	• Lucille Ball in the *I Love Lucy* episode "Job Switching/Candy Factory" • *City Slickers* • Eddie Murphy in *Trading Places* • Bill Murray in *Stripes* • Reese Witherspoon in *Legally Blonde*
What's Beyond In this Spolin-influenced sketch structure, characters do one thing and think about another. In other words, they deal with an emotional conflict unrelated to their current activity. In this type of scene, characters misdirect their emotions about what's happening elsewhere toward the characters in their company.	• Woody Allen's *Small Time Crooks* (He tries to burglarize a bank via the bakery next door. He nervously sells cookies in the front, while desperately trying to dig a tunnel in the back.) • *Mary Tyler Moore Show*, "Chuckles the Clown" episode. (Suppressing thoughts of the deceased, Mary laughs uncontrollably at his wake.)
Bathos High falutin' intentions get bogged down in the trivial and mundane.	• The Marx Brothers in *Duck Soup* • Monty Python's *Life of Brian*

Structure	Examples
Past Life The main character's *former* job or situation directly affects his reaction to his *new* surroundings. This structure is similar to Fish Out of Water, but more specific. It's great for monologues (e.g., a former stripper now works at NASA: "Countdown three baboom, two baboom, and one!"). As an improv exercise, two players are assigned a past vocation and a current "where" that is unfamiliar.	• John Belushi in *SNL*'s "Samurai" sketches • *The Coneheads* • *SNL's* "Robert Goulet Raps" • *3rd Rock from the Sun* • Tom Hanks in *Big*
Transposition of Temperament (Switch Emotions) In the Spolin exercise Take On Entering Player's Emotion, characters do just that. In this structure, two characters with opposite emotions end up switching to the other's emotion during the scene, and sometimes switching back again. Sometimes, just one character's trait contaminates the other.	• Abbott and Costello "Who's on First" • *SNL's* Richard Pryor in the "Racist Word Association Interview"
Character Flaw In this structure, a character's odd attribute is the *center* of conflict.	• *SNL's* Phil Hartman as the Anal-Retentive Chef • *SNL's* Gilda Radner as Emily Latella — an abrasive, deaf reporter • *SNL's* Jon Lovitz as the compulsive liar — "That's the ticket." • *SNL's* Will Ferrell as "The Man Who Cannot Modulate His Voice"

Structure	Examples
Deluge of Information In this structure, the focus is on the dialogue, which is chock full of specific nomenclature relating to the scene activity. The words just keep coming.	• Monty Python's "Spam" • Monty Python's "The Parrot Sketch"
Behind the Scenes of an Historical Event In this structure, we might see the Hindenburg crew smoking cigarettes before the explosion.	• *SNL's* "Napster Hearings" (Famous rockers give testimony to a glamour-hungry Senate.) • Sid Caesar's *Show of Shows'* sketch called "The Clock" (A famous Bavarian animated clock goes haywire.)
Sin, Recovery, Relapse This comedy structure features a character whose offensive character flaw surfaces three times. The character finally apologizes and vows to recover, but the flaw resurfaces.	• Martin Short as Comedy Central's Jiminy Glick • Abott and Costello radio broadcasts
Fantasy Sequence A character's own delusion takes over a scene, forcing an otherwise normal character into an absurd situation without his permission or control.	• Jim Carrey's *The Mask* • *Play It Again, Sam* • *The Wizard of Oz*
Genre Splicing In this structure, two social phenomena clash together for satiric effect.	• *Austin Powers* ('60s funk meets 007) • *Flintstones* (a prehistoric family meets modern psychology) • *The Beverly Hillbillies* (wealthy hicks meet Hollywood)

Structure	Examples
Split Screen/Give and Take In this Spolin-influenced structure, two separate scenes happen at the same time, with the focus on comparison. The stage left scene comments on and influences the stage right scene, and vice versa.	• *About Last Night* • *SNL's* "Beppe and Bushka" (Two spoiled female American office workers complain bitterly about trifling matters; Russian cleaning women top them with stories of homeland atrocities.)
Strict Parody *Parody* is the lampooning of a specific event, celebrity, work of art, or social phenomenon.	• *SNL's* news parody "Weekend Update" • *SNL's* "Elian, The Musical" • *SNL's* commercial "Happy Fun Ball" • *SNL's* celebrity and political impressions • *The Daily Show* with Jon Stewart
Mistaken Identity A person of one status or orientation is mistaken for a person of another status.	• *Being There* • *Nunsense* • *Waiting for Guffman* • *Bowfinger*
Animal Spines A character takes on the demeanor of a chosen animal, or they're possessed by the personality of another character.	• Rob Schneider's *The Animal* • *All of Me* (Lily Tomlin inhabits Steve Martin's body.)
Hidden Conflict A character has a hidden agenda, causing absurd behavior in a normal environment.	• *I Love Lucy's* "Jealous of Girl Dancer" episode
Scene on Scene (Flashback/Flash-forward) Insert flashbacks or flash-forwards into the middle of a scene. This allows you to justify an existing piece of information by revealing the past, or explore and heighten an existing predicament by revealing the future.	• *Groundhog Day* • Budget Rental Car's "What if" commercials (Advertising executives ruminate service changes and flash forward to their disastrous consequences.)

A Sketch Insurance Policy

Divide your sketch into three tiers: concept, structure, and performance. This will help you identify which part of your sketch is weak, and allow you to strengthen it.

Figure 3

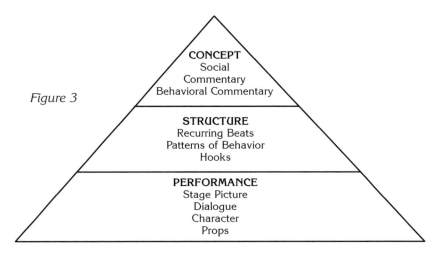

As shown in Figure 3, the concept tier is the idea or theme of the sketch. The structure tier is the series of events, or the repeating pattern of behavior in the sketch. The performance tier contains the dialogue, stage picture, character elements, and physical action that support the main action.

Here's an example:

Concept: *Lampoon the U.S. Senate's obsession with protocol. The Senate uses Robert's Rules of Order during an attack by space aliens.*
Structure: *The sketch follows Robert's Rules of Order. A senator calls for a motion to disarm the invaders. Another senator seconds the motion while laser sparks fly.*
Performance: *Senators hide behind their chairs, and aliens mock the senators. Aging Senator Strom Thurmond, unaware, continues to speak throughout the battle.*

Identify the weak tier in your sketch and strengthen it. Usually the high concept parodies are strong in social commentary but lacking in structure and performance. On the other hand, sketches that feature a lively character are often dismissed as "silly" because there isn't enough social commentary to support the concept tier.

The multiple layer approach keeps you from putting all your comedy eggs in one basket. It's a comedy insurance policy. If the sketch doesn't work on the concept level, it may work because the repeating action, costumes, dialogue, or stage picture is funny.

Storyboarding

The previous chapter introduced the idea of *storyboarding* your sketch idea *before* you write. That is, detail the dramatic action frame by frame and write the beats (bits) only, not the dialogue. It saves time and energy before you put pen to paper.

Storyboarding also works *after* you write a sketch. It helps to establish structure after you've written six pages of dialogue. It helps to pare down your sketch to a single, cohesive game. Here's an example of a sketch storyboard: *The Lion King* musical stage play had a ridiculously long run in L.A., making it ripe for lampooning:

Setup: *Announcer welcomes audience to the 823rd performance of* The Lion King. *Music starts.*

Bit 1: *First dancer leaps in with a life-size prop gazelle. Yawns. Second dancer enters with a gazelle. She wears headphones. Yawns.*
Third dancer shuffles in with gazelle under his arm. Exhausted, he chews gum and takes a cell phone call while performing.

Bit 2: *They dance their routines listlessly while talking and sharing the cell phone.*

Bit 3: *The caller tells the Third Dancer he's hired for another show! He exits elated!*
The Second Dancer cries and drops the gazelle onstage. Exits crying.

Blow: *The First Dancer stands alone while the musical number is still in progress.*
He opens the head of his prop gazelle, takes out a gun, and points it to his temple ...

Blackout

Storyboarding helped define the game in the sketch — the burned-out performers wrestle with the tedium of their show. Storyboarding helped focus the sketch on the physical activity and the heightened sequence of the game, *not on dialogue*.

If you can't put your completed sketch in storyboard format, it's not a sketch with a strong structure. In fact, it doesn't even make for good abstract theater. A sketch must contain a relatable pattern of events in which characters change in some way.

Use the storyboarding technique *before or after* you write your sketch as a way to boil down the dramatic action of your sketch into a list of actions without the dialogue. Outline the sketch first, beat by beat, bit by bit. Then assemble the bits in a heightened way with a twist on the ending. Add dialogue later. Don't fill the page with words if it doesn't support the underlying game. Delete the dialogue that doesn't support the structure of the bit sequence.

Elevator Speech

Another structural test is to reduce the action into an *elevator speech* — a thirty-second synopsis of the sketch, succinct enough to pitch during an elevator ride. This is a litmus test of your sketch's dramatic action.

You will probably resist this idea at first because it's very difficult to do. Once I worked with a player who said, "My sketch is not formulaic. It doesn't have a pattern. It's not that kind of sketch." Little did she know, it wasn't a sketch at all. It was a meandering, unstructured character study. The audience sat in confused silence each time she performed it. Had she pitched the sketch with an elevator speech, she would have seen that the sketch was unclear. Every good sketch, from *Monty Python* to *Mr. Show*, can be storyboarded or put into an elevator speech — even if it's a sketch about wordplay.

When you focus on the bits, suddenly you realize that dialogue is only one component of a great sketch. Yet, most new sketch writers feel obliged to start with a dialogue-based volley. "He says, then she

Tips

Comedy sketches always contain a recurring pattern of behavior or incidents.

Avoid incidents that happen by accident in a sketch. It's best if one character intentionally carries out an action on another.

146

says, and then he says … "

Sketches are usually four pages in standard typewritten script format. When I was a new sketch writer, I blathered on for six pages. I included too many characters, too much dialogue, too many games, blind alleys, too many points of focus, and plenty of arguing and name-calling. The elevator speech prevents this by forcing you to focus on the dramatic action. *What happens?* Even if your sketch is based on character, on an idiosyncratic verbal or physical game, or on no physical activity at all, if it's solid, you can turn it into an elevator speech.

> ***Bit 1:*** *Abbott tells Costello about an unusual baseball team with a player named "Who."*
> *Frustrated, Costello misunderstands "Who" is playing.*
> ***Bit 2:*** *Abbott tells Costello about a player named "What."*
> *More frustrated, Costello misunderstands "What."*
> ***Bit 3:*** *Abbott tells Costello about players named "Today," "Naturally," etc.*
> *More frustrated, Costello says "I don't give a darn."*
> ***Blow:*** *Abbott says, "I Don't Give A Darn is our short stop!" (A relapse.)*
> ***Blackout***

Storyboarding and elevator speeches allow you to flesh out a sketch without writing all four pages. A storyboard may only take you between five to thirty minutes to develop. Writing a sketch may take you three hours, after which you may realize you don't have an ending. Usually, you're better off storyboarding it first to see if you can extend the idea into a heightened sequence with a satisfying ending.

The Ending

If you can't think of an ending for your sketch, it's usually because the sketch doesn't have a singular through-line. Sketches should contain a clear, cohesive, singular game, which builds and heightens throughout the sketch. The ending is usually one of the following:

- *An unwelcome relapse* of an incident or character flaw
- *A final absurd instance* of an escalated problem
- *A switching of temperament*
- *A surprise emotion*
- *Taking on the other's character flaw (contamination)*
- *An unlikely agreement*
- *A hook*
- *An unexpected reversal of attitude*

Scattered Sketch

Find an ending to this scattered sketch:

1. Exhausted skiers in clumsy ski boots drag themselves across the floor to order a hot chocolate. They moan in pain as they walk to the counter.

2. Order-taker sits smugly behind the counter and will tell them when it's ready, but refuses to bring it to them.

3. Snow bunnies enter and entice the exhausted skiers to party, but they're too tired.

4. Order-taker tells the skiers that their hot chocolate is ready.

5. The skiers' boots begin to melt because they're too close to the fire.

6. The skiers crawl across the floor like conjoined crabs. They return to their tables, weeping and trying not to spill their drinks.

7. Ending?

Blackout

Difficult, isn't it? Was there a game? No. Was there a single point of focus? No. Now, find an ending to this clear progression:

1. Exhausted skiers in clumsy ski boots can barely walk across the floor to order a hot chocolate. They moan in pain as they walk to the counter.

2. Order-taker sits smugly behind the counter and will tell them when it's ready, but refuses to bring it to them.

3. Exhausted skiers drag themselves back to their table.

4. Order-taker smugly informs them their hot chocolate is ready, but refuses to help them.

5. The exhausted skiers crawl, moaning in pain, over to the hot chocolate stand to retrieve their drinks.

6. The skiers crawl across the floor, lying on top of one another like conjoined crabs. They return to their tables, weeping and trying not to spill their drinks.

7. Ending?

Blackout

Ending: The order-taker tells them the price of the drinks, implying they forgot to pay— they'll have to crawl all the way back!

There was very little dialogue in that sketch which The Groundlings performed in 2002. It featured a clear repeating pattern of events with a strong ending and had audiences in stitches for four solid minutes.

So, to find an ending, storyboard the sketch without dialogue. Define what happens in each beat. Define the pattern of action. If each beat has the same singular focus, an ending is merely an exercise in heightening, reversing, revisiting the problem, or revealing unlikely information.

The *final blow* (or *button*) is a final piece of information that caps the scene. Don't go for the obvious ending. Search vigorously for a less obvious, secondary, or unique option.

New sketch writers often rely heavily on blows that reveal a surprise who, what, or where. However, if the information is from left field, the audience won't buy it. Usually, a final blow is a last, heightened iteration of the game.

Trimming Your Dialogue

Remove extraneous words in dialogue, as shown below.

Dad: (Confidently) *Tommy, ~~there's something I am wondering about whether or not to tell you. I guess I should, although you may resist it. At the risk of sounding like an over-involved parent who's forcing you to be something you're not ready to be, I'll say~~ you're gay. And that's wonderful! Your mother and I are hosting a coming-out party for you on Saturday. ~~I'm happy to say,~~ I'm going to stock the fridge with Seagram's Golden Wine Coolers.*

- *Write in short sentences.* Heighten the word selection.
- *Cut the extraneous words.* Cut stagnant lines like "I'm bored." Cut lines telling the emotion.
- *The character should show his history,* but not tell it.
- *Place the punch word with "oomph"* at the end of a sentence.
- *Replace dialogue that tells the emotion with stage directions,* e.g., *(blithely)*.

Just for fun, take an early sketch you've written and cut it down to the essentials — the bits. Surprise yourself with how much of the dialogue you can cut because it is superfluous to the game.

Reveals

Radio and TV ads often use *reveals* which reverse assumed foundational information by replacing it with the unexpected.

SCENE: Two men work on defusing a time bomb.

Player One: *I suggest you cut the red wire before the blue one, otherwise we'll explode.*

Player Two: *Say, good job, FBI man!*

Player One: *I'm not in the FBI, but I did stay at a Holiday Inn Express last night.*

We first assume the subject is an FBI agent, but we learn later that he's not.

Reveals can expose any piece of information, usually who,

what, where, the character's emotion, stage picture, or point of view, *but only after each is previously established by assumption.*

Observe the use of reveals in this radio commercial:

Boss: (Blows whistle.) *All right, team, huddle up!*

Ted: Sir, it's unusual for accountants to huddle up in a conference room. [Reveal: Where, Who]

Boss: Well, we need a team mentality. We're gonna score with our clients using our new Xtreme software!

Ted: Sir, I'm a team player, but do you have to pat my butt?" [Reveal: What]

Boss: Oh, sorry. Our Xtreme accounting software is compatible with our legacy system, and easily integrates with our email. So, let's go accounting team!

Ted: Sir, let's hire these cheerleaders full time! [Reveal: Stage picture]

Be careful — if the reveal is too big a leap of absurdity, the audience won't buy it, and the reveal falls flat. In addition, if you reveal unlikely information without carefully setting up the assumed information first, the gag is lost.

Reveals commonly appear at the end of the scene as a final blow. You may notice that reveals are borderline negations and don't work in improv — improv requires instant excessive agreement in order to set up a blind scene from scratch.

Also, don't confuse reveals with the simple exposing of interesting information. Reveals reverse primary information that is already established (or strongly assumed) in the sketch.

Parodies Are Easy. Comedy Is Hard.

When I began writing sketch comedy I hid behind parodies of commercials and TV talk shows — they were easy to write. Commercials and talk shows have a beginning, middle, and end built in. There's no need to build a foundation from scratch — it's already there. Commercial parodies have an assumed introduction: "Are you tired of ... ," an informational midsection, and a final 1-800 number at the end. Talk show parodies start with an introduction, celebrity impersonations, and a ubiquitous "Join us next week when our guest will be … ." Pretty formulaic.

Parodies of TV shows and film are a little bit more challenging because you must establish a game, just like a standard sketch. Give your parody some staying power by targeting the media that deserve it — those with the most brazen vice or folly.

It's much more lucrative to create fictional characters than to parody celebrities. When you own the character, you can freely adapt it for film, without walking on legal egg shells with the disgruntled celebrity that you impersonate. *Wayne's World, Pee Wee's Big Adventure,* and *The Blues Brothers* are successful films with huge merchandising revenues based on fictional characters developed from scratch. After all, how many films or action figures have you seen that parody specific, real-life celebrities or political figures? My attorney says, "Not many."

Summary

- *Use standardized criticisms* — it's less painful.
- *Study the common sketch structures.* It will give you a point of reference for your own sketches and help you find an ending.
- *Learn the tricks of the trade.* Practice the three-tiered approach, storyboarding, creating endings, trimming dialogue, and using reveals.

Chapter 28
Getting Your Sketch on Its Feet

"I was in a sketch group, and a fellow player handed me an Abbott and Costello spoof. I thought it was pretty dry, so I dismissed it. When we got it on its feet, it was amazing. Turned out to be the hit of our sketch show."
— Author's Journal, November 3, 2001

Tricks of the Trade

On Your Feet!

Don't judge a sketch by a first reading alone. A sketch takes on a new life once it gets on its feet. Great sketches often look dull on paper until players add life to them with character and emotion.

Props and Costumes

For sketches, select costume pieces that evoke the essence of your character. Use props sparingly and only if they are essential for the scene's action. If you add too many, you'll shift the point of focus of the scene away from its original intention. Use labels to describe the who, what, and where. The audience's willing suspension of disbelief will fill in the rest.

Shtick

Bits of business and physical interplay between characters — character shtick — can bring out laughs, as long as they support the scene's main action. Harvest the bits from the text, the interplay, the dramatic action, and character attributes. Don't lay on extraneous bits, like so many Duncan Hines Cupcake Sprinkles.

Lib a Little, Laugh a Little

In rehearsal, an *ad lib* (improvised line) can help accentuate a comic bit. In performance, an ad lib can freshen a stale scene. Be careful — if you didn't write the scene, your ad lib might step on the writer's toes. Too much ad lib may shift the focus of the scene or throw off the timing. So, avoid surprising your scene partners or the writers with an unsolicited ad lib in performance. Test the waters in rehearsal. Get a feel for the required level of improvisational input and adjust accordingly.

How Dare You Give Me Line Readings!

Unlike most dramatic actors, many comedians welcome line readings. When you play with the rhythm of your lines, you maximize the comic effect. Timing is everything. Be open to suggestions and you will reap the rewards.

No Small Roles

A well-written sketch is nothing without actors who are able to bring zest and flourish to the roles. Often in introductory writing classes, you will have to make do with timid actors who require coaching or who cannot convey some of the emotions or character complexity you've written. In advanced classes, the casting job gets easier because actors are more experienced and committed.

Take stock: As you prepare for performance, are you lending an ear to which sketches your fellow players like? Are you incorporating your instructor's (director's) feedback? Are you remembering to develop strong characters in your sketches, even in the final weeks before your performance? Are you learning to navigate the tricky process of sketch collaboration?

Writing and Working with Others

Adapt or Die

Your sketch is not your "baby." When you spend too much time with a sketch, you become attached to it, and you resist good suggestions for change. Always be open to suggestions from the director and skilled players you trust. Comedy requires teamwork, fresh perspective, and willingness to change. Remember, hang together or you'll all hang separately, in costume.

Positive Feedback

In most theater companies, you develop a bond with your fellow players over the months or years during production. In class, however, you only have six to twelve weeks — barely enough time to type the contact list into your PDA. What should be a nurturing ensemble is really more like a newly formed theater troupe. Be patient. Recognize the skills in each fellow player. Set aside time to get to know them. Who knows? You may work for the rest of your life with these people.

Be Professional

Show a professional attitude toward your fellow sketch players, especially if you are in a competitive program and you're vying for a spot in a premiere comedy troupe. Don't talk behind people's backs. Keep a positive attitude in rehearsals. If you become a paid writer or collaborator, you'll have to be diplomatic in delivering feedback and criticism. Start now.

Writing in Groups without Killing Each Other

Collaboration is stressful, especially when you're paired with students who have never written before.

Here are the traps you'll fall into:

- *The Coffee Shop Flare-up.* All players, seated at a cramped table in a coffee shop, arguing about the dialogue, without first improvising and storyboarding the sketch.
- *The "Omnipotent Scribe" Syndrome.* Your writing partner sits at the keyboard, transcribing the ideas and dialogue you offer, but unilaterally edits your ideas right in front of you. Curiously, all his own ideas stay in. Better to write alone and compare together.
- *"My character wouldn't say that!"* Some actors write dialogue based on their character's inner monologue, without regard to the needs of the scene structure.
- *"My line is my real estate!"* Performers in a crowded class feel pressure to stand out and get noticed. As a result, they pump up their dialogue and character, shifting the entire focus of a scene.

Use this method of collaboration after the improv performance:

1. *Write alone.* After the improvisation, and after you receive the director's feedback, each player rewrites his own separate version of the sketch.

2. *Compare and perform.* Reassemble. Read all versions. Get each version on its feet. See what works. Agree, in general, about which parts to include and which not to include.

3. *Cut and paste alone.* Everyone retreats and individually hones the sketch. Each player cuts and pastes the best structure, character, and dialogue from all versions into a modified draft.

4. *Repeat*, starting with number 2.

You may get lucky and find someone with whom you work well and whose style matches your own. Hang on to them. Develop a partnership with them for future projects.

When presenting your draft sketch to others in the group, read the whole thing aloud to them rather than having them read it cold in a group. This way, you can sell it. You control the delivery. The players who read your sketch may not be good cold readers. Their reading affects the timing and presentation of your sketch. Reading it yourself allows the participants to visualize it, and you control how well it is presented.

Sometimes the best sketch writing is knowing when to do nothing. If a writing partner wrote something great, go with it. Step back. Don't fight to get your own dialogue into a sketch that already works. Save your energy for the next sketch.

Getting Stuck with Weak Writing Partners

Comedy writing classes challenge you to collaborate under absurd constraints. Some fellow students have never written sketch comedy before. Some are weak improvisers or actors. Some misguided players demand to include special phrases they've coined, whether or not it serves the scene. There is only one place that is more absurd in its constraints — the real world.

> *"I had my first paid writing gig today. I wrote dialogue for a*
> *restaurant spot — a cartoon grill chasing raw vegetables.*
> *The producer said, 'Keep it light and breezy.'"*
> *— Author's Journal, November 3, 2001*

That's right, writing classes closely parallel the real world writing assignments that you'll get — impossible character combinations, requisite plot twists, egotistical writers with creative control, actors who want to reword the lines. Be flexible.

Ask these questions of your writing partners to help them focus:

- *What is the point of focus* of the scene?
- *What is the game* in this scene?
- *Can you storyboard the scene* for us without dialogue? What happens first, second, third?
- *What are your characters' objectives,* and what do they want from each other?

Preparing for Performance

Previews

In open run sketch shows, it's difficult to know which sketches work until you perform previews. After the preview, your director will change the order and replace soft sketches before you open. Time is the true test. If a sketch bombs for two audiences, you can be sure it needs an overhaul or replacement. Perform, get feedback, and edit. This iterative process works for sketch shows, sitcoms, standup, and even film.

Stealthy comedy theaters test new material weekly by sandwiching it between proven sketches, same as standup. Therefore, if you only have one show date, you're at a disadvantage.

Don't blame the audience for not laughing. Replace, rework, tweak, and hone. If you're developing an open run sketch show, consider your play list to be an ever-changing lineup that you reinvent each week.

Setting the Show

In your final rehearsal the director solidifies or *sets* the sketch. Perform it as rehearsed — don't add "surprises" in performance. Don't add any new props, costumes, or wild changes in character that may shift the scene's focus. Your director and fellow players expect you to perform it as planned, adding a nuance of fresh discovery.

Always Employ an Experienced Director

As you near the end of your writing class, your instructor fills the role of show director. He will select scenes based on quality, variety, and how well they showcase student talent. There's no trick to being well represented here. Put forth your best writing on every single sketch. If a director selects a sketch you dislike, work with your partner to revise it until you are satisfied with it and review the changes with the director.

> *"We won't need a director. It's a tight-knit group."*
> — Author's Journal, November 1, 2001

If you're assembling a sketch show outside of class, you will need an experienced director because he keeps everyone in the troupe humble. He avoids personal influence, weeds out weak sketches, and nurtures the strong ones. He selects scenes that balance and shape the production. Have you ever worked *without* a director and an influential player refused to cut his weak sketch? It's a no-win situation, and everyone in the show suffers. A strong director can squelch the dictators and nurture the meek. However, all players in the group must grant the director full authority before the process begins.

> *"Holy God, we need a director. Players aren't being objective about their own material. Egos abound!"*
> — Author's Journal, November 2, 2001

Arrange to have your sketch show performance videotaped so that you can review what worked and what didn't. The learning process continues, performance after performance, sketch after sketch.

Summary
- *Get the sketch on its feet.*
- *Use previews* as a way to test and tweak your show.
- *Employ an experienced director;* incorporate feedback.

Chapter 29

Sketch Writing Wrap-Up

The Writer's Voice

Once you sharpen your sketch writing skills, take a step back and look at your sketch content as a whole. What messages are your sketches conveying? Do they have any lasting significance? Do they contain any political commentary? Do they contain social, behavioral, or cultural commentary that will last beyond the performance? Any philosophical or spiritual significance?

Although you may have become a writer via your acting aspirations, recognize the power behind the pen. You have the power to influence wide-reaching audiences and a responsibility to explore issues beyond the standard *Fantasy Island* parody. Dig deep.

Take stock: The improv, character, and writing techniques you've learned will serve you long after your classes have finished. Your skills will help you advance beyond the three-minute medium of improv and sketch comedy. Try your hand at developing a short film or play.

Keep in contact with the classmates you trust. The writing partners you have today can grow into professional, even nurturing partnerships in the future.

Whether or not you beat the odds and perform in a main stage company, you will have succeeded. The actor who writes is a stronger, smarter performer. The writer who collaborates can lead and follow. The artist who learns from his fellow players builds partnerships that last a lifetime.

Summary

- *Use your life as your wellspring of comedy material.*
- *Use improv to write; study the understructure of sketch comedy.*
- *Broaden your range of material.* Dig deep to create political, social, and even philosophical content.

Appendix

Exercises

The following exercises are grouped by type. Any three-hour class session usually covers a sampling of exercises like the ones categorized below. (For example, a Beginning Improv session may include a couple of warm-up exercises, a few Group Mind exercises, a couple of exercises from the Practice Adding the Foundation category, and an exercise from Beginning Improv Exercises.)

My intention is to capture the essence of the types of exercises at most schools, not re-create a syllabus or performance lineup. Almost all of the exercises featured in this book are in common use at most schools.

An abbreviation at the end of each exercise indicates which schools currently use it. It's difficult to track the origin and historical use of improv exercises. However, if you have information about attributing an exercise, please feel free to contact me at BillLynn2004@yahoo.com. Also, for a history of long form handles, I recommend Rob Kozlowski's book *The Art of Chicago Improv: Short Cuts to Long-Form Improvisation* (Portsmouth, NJ:Heinemann, 2002).

ES	The Empty Stage, Los Angeles
G	The Groundlings
IO	ImprovOlympic
KK	Kip King On-Camera Acting Technique
LATS	L.A. Theater Sports
PW	Player's Workshop
SC	The Second City
SNL	Saturday Night Live
UIUC	University of Illinois, Urbana/Champaign
O	Other venues
Common	Common to many theater schools
*	Indicates a mutation of the exercise is performed at the school noted.

Sample Audition Exercises

Audition Exercise: One Word Story
 (a.k.a. *One Word at a Time* or *Word at a Time Story)*
In this exercise, players stand in a circle, and each student, in order, adds one word to build normal sentences that build a logical story. "The … cat … walked … over … to … the … _____." Avoid adding strange words. Don't try to be funny; this is a test of your logic and normalcy. Just work with your fellow players to tell a logical story, one word at a time.

Story/Story (a.k.a. *Conducted Story)*
 (My first contact — The Groundlings)
Group. Six players form a line. The instructor selects a story topic or genre like "Pulp Fiction" or "Romance Novel" and points to a player, who starts the story. The instructor, like a conductor, points to another player, who must continue the story just where the previous player left off, seamlessly. Even mid-syllable. Variation: each player is assigned a different emotion before the story begins. (Focus: give and take, listening, "Yes anding.") Current usage: Common.

*"Hello, I'm … " (*a.k.a. *Superheroes)* (My first contact —
 Kip King's On-Camera Acting Technique class)
Solo exercise. In this advanced exercise, the instructor selects a player and randomly assigns a title, like "Litigation Man," or "King of Burning Rubber." The instructor asks the player to extemporize a two-minute monologue as that character. The monologue begins and ends with the identifying phrase, "Hello, I'm …" and the player's title. Players use the foundation, who, what, and where. The more specific the character is about his attitudes and what he is doing, the better. Advanced players develop a character with a facade hiding his true feelings, or build in a theme that is universally human and recognizable to all of us, e.g., a superhero with a fear of failure. (Focus: commitment, stage presence, foundation, emotion, finding a character game.) Current usage: Common.

A Simple Three-Person Improv Scene
(My first contact — The Second City, Los Angeles audition)
This improv exercise is a simple three-person scene with a given work location, e.g., the security office of "Camp Snoopy" at the Mall of America. Instructors can tell if you've studied improvisation before. (Focus: listening, "Yes anding," agreement, stage presence, building the foundation, growing the game.) Current usage: Common.

Warm-up Exercises

Trust Lift (My first contact — University of Illinois, Urbana/Champaign)
Group. Players gather in a circle around Player One. Player One makes his body rigid. Remaining players lift Player One in the air, shoulder high. Players walk around with the elevated player in tow and gently place him down. (Focus: trust, give and take, physical warm-up.) Current usage: Common.

Simon Says
Group. The classic children's game. A leader gives commands to a group, who must follow only those commands that begin with the words "Simon says." When players falter, the instructor eliminates them from the game. (Focus: listening, concentrating, following a leader, mirroring.) Current usage: Common.

Tug of War — Imaginary Rope (My first contact — Viola Spolin's writings)
Group. All players divide into two teams. Upon the instructor's command, the teams play tug of war with an imaginary rope. As the teams pull, the rope must retain its form. This is harder than it sounds. Teams must agree to give and take, carefully observing the other players in order to maintain the integrity of the mimed rope. Eventually, players realize that in order to make a scene work, they must give up control and act as part of a whole. (Focus: group object work, give and take, listening, concentrating, following a leader, mirroring.) Current usage: Common.

Machines (My first contact — University of Illinois, Urbana/Champaign)

Five to six players. In this classic theater game, Player One starts alone onstage, making a repeating rhythmic motion with sound, representing a part of a machine, e.g., a treasury printing press. The next player joins in as an adjacent part, adding a different repeating motion with sound, physically connected with Player One in some way. When all players have joined, the instructor suggests an emotion, and the machine takes on the new emotion, changing the rhythm, tempo, and attitude. (Focus: rhythm, group awareness, listening, agreement, exploring emotions, stage picture.) Current usage: Common.

Mirror Exercise in Pairs (My first contact — Viola Spolin's writings)

Two players mirror each other. Player One takes the lead, silently moving in slow motion. Player Two follows. Then, they switch. Eventually they both follow each other together. (Focus: give and take, listening.) Current usage: Common.

Exercises for Group Mind and Rolodexing

One to Twenty in a Circle (My first contact — IO Los Angeles)

Group. In a circle, the group counts to twenty. Players take turns adding the next number in sequence but without knowing who will say the next number. The emphasis is on a seamless flow of numbers. Players should use their peripheral vision and extrasensory perception. If there's a mistake, players start over. (Focus: give and take, listening, trust.) Current usage: Common.

Pass the Ball (**Variations:** *Pass the Object, Word, etc.)*
  (My first contact — IO Los Angeles)

Group. In a circle, each person passes a ball to the next player, who must retain the ball's properties as it is handed to him (e.g., size, weight, feel, temperature, etc.). Once Player One passes the ball, Player Two gradually changes the ball's properties and passes it to the next player. (Focus: give and take, listening, watching.) Current usage: Common.

Bunny, Bunny, BUNNY! (My first contact — The Groundlings.)

Group. In a circle, Player One quickly repeats "Bunny, bunny, bunny," miming bunny ears with both his hands, with players on his left and right adding single ears on his left and right, respectively. Player One shouts a final "Bunny!" to another random player (Player Two) in the circle. Player Two does the same — she becomes the bunny, miming the ears, with players on her left and right adding single ears on her left and right. Player Two quickly repeats "Bunny, bunny, bunny," passing the bunny to a third random player. The instructor eliminates any player who forgets to become the bunny ears, leaving only the remaining players. The competition continues, faster and faster, until only one player remains and is crowned the winner. (Focus: concentration, rhythm, group awareness.) Current usage: Common.

Zip Zap Zop (**And variations**) (My first contact — IO Los Angeles)

Group. Similar to "Bunny, Bunny, BUNNY," this is a rapid-fire team exercise. All players stand in a circle. The group should sound like a continuous peal of "Zip," "Zap," "Zop!" as they pass the "Zip" in rapid succession in a random pattern around the circle. Here's how it works: As if they were tossing a ball randomly around the circle, Player One claps once and shouts a "Zip" to a second random player, who claps once and shouts a "Zap" to a third random player. Player Three claps once and shouts a "Zop" to a fourth random player, and then it repeats in random order around the circle. Variation: instead of "Zip," "Zap," "Zop!" each player adds a single word to create a logical sentence. (Focus: non-verbal communication, listening.) Current usage: Common.

Circle Pulse — (My first contact — University of Illinois, Urbana/Champaign)

Group. All hold hands in a circle. The instructor designates a player to squeeze the hand once of the player to his right, who in turn squeezes the hand to her right, creating a chain reaction around the circle. Later, players can try sending two pulses. Then, send pulses in opposite directions. (Focus: waiting for an impulse, listening, concentration.) Current usage: Common.

Killer (a.k.a. J'Accuse) (My first contact — The Groundlings)
Group. Before the game starts, the instructor secretly assigns one player as a "Killer." The Killer's objective is to "kill" everyone with a surreptitious wink of an eye, without being discovered. The players walk randomly around the stage in silence. Each time the designated Killer winks at another player in passing, the recipient must die in a dramatic way and fall to the floor. (The Killer must wink surreptitiously to avoid being discovered.) All players try to identify who the Killer is, without being winked at first. If a player thinks he knows who the Killer is, he shouts the Killer's name and "J'Accuse!" If a player guesses *incorrectly* who the Killer is, the *player* must die. If a player *correctly* identifies the Killer, the Killer must die. (Focus: concentration, commitment, group awareness.) Current usage: Common.

Morph a Word/Morph an Object
  (My first contact — Viola Spolin's writings)
Group. With the group standing in a circle, Player One starts with a word like "butter," and playfully morphs the word into another word with successive iterations, e.g., butter blatter blatta blazza belaza belacka Binaca. The next person in the circle takes the newly formed word "Binaca" and morphs it into another word, and passes it to the next player. A variation on this game, Morph an Object, asks players to create object work and pass it to the next player, who physically morphs it into another object. (Focus: wordplay, object work, commitment.) Current usage: Common.

Two Xs Walk into a Bar (My first contact — Players Workshop)
Group. All players walk freely around the stage. The instructor selects a player and a random object, like "celery." The selected player boldly tells a standardized joke with an improvised punch line, delivering it with confidence and zest. The player fills in the blanks: "A piece of celery walks into a bar, and the bartender says 'we don't serve celery' and the piece of celery says, 'That's it! I'm gonna stalk you.'" Usually the punch line is a pun pertaining to the object. (Focus: rolodexing, word play, commitment.) Current usage: Common.

Topic Firing Line (a.k.a. *Ru Ru Ru*)

(My first contact — The Groundlings)

Group. In this exercise developed by George McGrath of The Groundlings, all players line up for a rapid-fire competition. The instructor calls out a category, like "soap operas," and each player in turn steps forward with commitment and boldly announces the made-up name of a soap opera, e.g., "Brunch and Divorce" or "Lipstick on the World's Collar." The instructor eliminates players who repeat, hesitate, lack commitment, or break character. Some instructors change the topic midstream. As a variation, the instructor calls out an absurdly complicated or technical question and the players must answer briefly, resolutely, and confidently. (Focus: rolodexing, concentration, commitment to the ridiculous.) Current usage: Common.

Building a Story

"Yes, and" (a.k.a. *Story/Story*)

(My first contact — IO Los Angeles)

Two players sit facing each other. Player One starts a story with a single, short sentence in past tense, like "I went golfing." Player Two confirms what his partner says and adds to it, starting with the words "Yes, and you ... ." Player One continues with "Yes, and I ... " and so on. Players should keep the sentences short, on the same topic, and establish themes in the story. Players should get a feel for when to add detail, and when to move on. The instructor ends the story at his discretion, usually at the one- or two-minute mark. (Focus: listening, give and take, finding a game.) Current usage: Common.

"That means ... " (My first contact — The Groundlings)

Two players. To practice exploring and heightening, play a variation on the "Yes and" exercise called "That Means," where the players substitute "That means ..." for "Yes and" in order to build a premise. Two players sit opposite one another and add information to build a story. This exercise focuses players on creating a single action together, reinforcing the meaning behind the other's statement, with

166

an automatic exploring and heightening, creating an instant game. Both players agree on what the other "means." Players should perform the "Yes and" exercise first.

Player One: I gambled in Vegas.

Player Two: That means you risked a lot of money.

Player One: That means I lost big.

Player Two: That means you are staying temporarily in your ex-wife's house.

Player One: That means I am under her thumb.

Player Two: That means you are humiliated.

Player One: That means I am her house slave.

Player Two: That means you are your children's butler.

(Focus: listening, give and take, finding a game, accepting the intended offer.) Current usage: Common.

Practice Object Work

Everyday Task (My first contact — University of Illinois, Urbana/Champaign)

Solo exercise. This is the classic actor's exercise developed by Uta Hagen. A player prepares and performs a scene to practice using object work at the fourth wall. He re-creates the essence of a simple daily routine, without words. The way he enters and handles his imaginary props reveals information about the character, its history, environment, and point of view. The player should include the interesting aspects of the daily routine and edit out the dull parts. This distillation process is the essence of comedy. (Focus: object work, fourth wall, being natural, distilling the essence of behavior.) Current usage: Common.

Practice Adding the Foundation

Homework: List Fifty Emotions
(My first contact — The Groundlings)

Solo exercise. Outside of class, a player writes down fifty words describing emotions. Sad, happy, angry, frightened, etc. All

167

emotions are variations on the basic four. Then the player writes down examples of "labels:" *emotions* (giddy, enraged, content), *attributes* (jealous, stingy, pompous), and *credentials* (prosecuting attorney, green grocer, Fellow in the study of allergies). Labels help to develop the character's point of view and advance the scene. (Focus: emotion, labeling.) Current usage: Common.

Add Info Lineup (a.k.a. *Short Scenes* or *Two Lines)*
  (My first contact — The Groundlings)

In this exercise created by Phyllis Katz and Cathy Shambley of The Groundlings, players assemble into two lines. Players from each line pair up with a player from the other line. The first pair starts by observing each other's silent object work. In conversation, Player One identifies his partner by name or occupation (who), and then identifies what they are doing (what). Player Two responds in conversation and identifies Player One by name (who) and where they are (where):

> **Player One:** *Who. What.*
> **Player Two:** *Who. Where.*

Once the information is out, the scene is finished. The next pair of players in line begin a new scene. Many variations. (Focus: adding foundation.) Current usage: Common.

Add Info Lineup/Short Scenes — *Other Variations*
  (My first contact — The Groundlings)

Attribute on Paper — each player has a piece of paper with a character "attitude" on it to color the scene. *Lame Player* — one player adds *all* the foundation information; the other player "Yes ands" the information. *Freeze Tag* — players call "freeze" and replace the two existing players, and create a new scene, assuming the previous players' exact body positions. (Players must use lots of body movement and object work in each scene.) In *Mirror Your Partner*, two players start object work and mimic the other's emotion before the scene begins. In this variation, it isn't critical which player adds which information, or in what order. (Focus: foundation, "Yes and," positive start.) Current usage: Common.

Homework: Saying Who, What, and Where

Solo exercise. Outside of class, a player practices setting up scenes with a single sentence of expository dialogue that labels who, what, and where. Later, the player practices responding to the setup lines. (Focus: foundation, "Yes and.") Current usage: Common.

Short Scenes Based on a Morphed Passed Word
(My first contact — IO Los Angeles)

Group. With all players in a circle, Player One passes a single word to the next player in the circle, e.g., "Celery." The next player in the circle creates a word based on the last letter of "celery." "Yardstick." The next player's word starts with *k*, and so on. The instructor randomly selects certain words upon which to base a quick two-person scene, performed in the center of the circle. It helps if players start the scene in an interesting physical position. (Focus: wordplay, foundation, "Yes and.") Current usage: IO, O.

Scene Tops (My first contact — The Groundlings)

Two players. In this exercise created by Patrick Bristow of The Groundlings, the focus is on the first critical moments of an improv between receiving a suggestion for a scene and establishing the foundation. The instructor gives the two players a suggestion for a scene: a specific location or a relationship. For advanced players, the instructor gives an enigmatic suggestion like the word "blue" or the expression "the Jazz Age." The instructor briefly reviews the suggestion with the student audience, calls for a blackout and applause to start the scene. During these critical pre-scene moments, the players focus on letting the suggestion wash over them, creating a visual picture in their minds of the scene, free associating, and rolodexing the specific mental and sensory images of the environment and activity they're about to create. The players allow their unique, intuitive images to viscerally incite them to create a dramatic stage picture, explore a fully committed emotion, and perform object work that connects them with their partner as they establish the foundation of the scene. When the scene is established, the instructor calls "*scenus interruptus,*" stopping the scene, and giving them a new suggestion to repeat the process. The two players perform five or ten "scene tops," giving them plenty of practice in the free association before scenes begin, a skill critical to establishing unique scenes from the actor's wellspring of personal images. (Focus: rolodexing, mental images, establishing the foundation.) Current usage: G.

Beginning Improv Scenes

Alphabet Game (My first contact — Players Workshop)
Two players. Players are given a location, like an army barracks, and they build a scene, starting their sentences with the next letter in the alphabet.

> **Player One:** <u>A</u>ll right, Sgt. Finkelstein, here's your mail.
> **Player Two:** <u>B</u>orscht from my Jewish mother who worries about me being in the army!

Players must commit to and justify the words they say, even if the words are somewhat random. In addition, players must build the foundation, as usual. (Focus: justifying, new choice.) Current usage: Common.

Stand, Sit, Kneel (My first contact — The Groundlings)
Three players. With only a given "where," three players set up a scene as usual. However, there is only one rule: at any given time, only one player must be standing, one must be sitting, and one must be kneeling. If the kneeling player stands, all players must adjust so that they comply with the rule. This creates an ever-changing stage picture. As the stage picture changes, the players justify it by adding new information. The new information, in turn, forces the players to change the stage picture. Yin and yang. (Focus: stage picture, justifying.) Current usage: Common.

New Choice (My first contact — University of Illinois, Urbana/Champaign)
Two players. Develop a scene with a given what or where. The instructor calls "new choice," forcing the player who is talking to

finish his sentence with a new random piece of information.

> *Player One:* In the early morning, I like pancakes.
> *Instructor:* New choice!
> *Player One:* In the early morning, I like striptease.
> *Instructor:* New choice!
> *Player One:* In the early morning, I like science experiments! I like to see explosions before I head off to my boring accounting job.

Players add new, random information and justify it. They must make the new information make sense in the context of the current scene. (Focus: avoiding the urge to plan ahead, making bold choices, justifying, "Yes and.") Current usage: Common.

First Line/Last Line (My first contact — Kip King On-Camera Acting Technique class)

Two players. Before the scene starts, the instructor offers a given location, like a meat locker, and assigns the first and last lines of the scene. The players have to fill in the rest. For example, Player One gets a first line, based on the location, like "I'm sorry I locked us in the meat locker, Boss." Player Two gets the unrelated last line of the scene, like "Clog dancing means so much more to me, now!" The players must get from point A to point B in three minutes. The last line is completely absurd and unrelated to the first. The only way the players will arrive at the last line in a logical way is to fully commit, make bold choices, and continually add new information to the scene: who, what, and where, object work, changing the stage picture, exploring their relationship, changing the tempo, and becoming emotional. The players must justify the absurd information and make sense of it. The instructor calls out "Thirty seconds!" as the players near the three-minute mark. This turns up the heat, forcing the players to heighten their predicament to logically arrive at the absurd last line. (Focus: commitment, justifying, foundation, emotion, object work, character, changing the stage picture.) Current usage: KK, G, O.

"Taking the Plunge" into Character Essences

Mood Swing (Based on a Viola Spolin exercise on emotions)

Solo exercise. Outside of class, the player sits in a chair across from a mirror. The player begins telling a story about his most recent vacation. The player speaks as himself and retells the incidents of the vacation, naturally and sincerely. During the story, the player intermittently opens six pieces of paper with an emotion pre-written on each. The player adopts each emotion as he continues his story, justifying the new emotion, and at the end, recovering to the neutral state with which he began. (Focus: emotional range, observing your expressions in the mirror, maintaining honesty in emotion, allowing emotion to affect story content, allowing emotion to build point of view.) Current usage: O.

Object Work Creates a Character
(My first contact — Viola Spolin's writings)

Group. In this exercise based on a Spolin classic, players walk randomly around the stage. The instructor assigns a "who," like George Washington. The players continue moving, explore the specific objects relating to a task in this person's environment, conjure an emotion, and become the character. This is not just movement for movement's sake, not gesturing, but actually doing a task that links this person to this location, for a high-stakes, emotional reason. (Focus: creating character essence, object work, generating emotion.) Current usage: Common.

Giants (a.k.a. Character Walk or Spolin's Space Walk/Attitude)
(My first contact — Viola Spolin's writings)

Solo. This exercise was originated by Spolin and developed by Gary Austin of The Groundlings. A selected player walks randomly around the stage. The instructor calls out a single character or celebrity (e.g., "defense attorney" or "Pope"). The player assumes the physicality of the character, based on his personal images. As the player discovers the character's walk, he begins to speak as the character, and plays the given character *large* — with utter commitment, finding a heightened emotion, as if he is a giant. The

172

player must create object work that is *specific* and germane to the environment of that character (not just gestures). Allow the object work to trigger a specific, heightened emotion or attitude. Below is a simple example. Current usage: G.

> *Priest:* (Picking up a martini glass) *I never thought I would say an impromptu Mass at the Playboy mansion. Let's see, I'll use this martini glass for a chalice ... Waiter! Let me have a handful of that pita appetizer ...*

Either Or (a.k.a. *Opposite Characters*)
(My first contact — The Groundlings)
Group. Players walk randomly around the stage. The instructor calls out two opposite characters, e.g., first a Republican and then a Democrat. Players develop the first character by finding object work, adding emotion, making it specific, and developing a distinct physical and vocal demeanor. Then, players develop the second, opposite character the same way. The instructor tells the players to switch back and forth, contrasting the two. Because the players perform simultaneously, with everyone talking at once, players feel free to commit to their bold choices. (Focus: developing character essence, character range, character contrast.) Current usage: Common.

Characters from a Random Suggestion ... Like a Blender

The Leading Authority (a.k.a. *Expert Talker*)
(My first contact — University of Illinois, Urbana/Champaign)
Solo exercise. In this exercise developed by Gary Austin, the instructor picks a player and assigns him the character of a specialist in a given field. The player improvises a character who talks confidently, knowledgeably, and emotionally about his complex topic, as if giving a speech at a seminar. The player adds a who, what, where, and object work. After the informational speech, the instructor opens the floor to questions from the other players in the audience. (Focus: developing character game.) Current usage: G*.

Characters from Animal Spines or Household Objects
(My first contact — Viola Spolin's writings)

Group. Based on the Spolin exercise "Animal Spines," players walk randomly around the stage. The instructor calls out a suggestion: an animal or an object. Players first physically morph into the animal or object. Then players morph into walking, talking human characters, retaining the properties of that animal or object. Any impetus (planets, villains, pets) can be the starting point for a character. Briefly interact with others in the group. (Focus: developing character essence, developing point of view.) Current usage: UIUC, IO, SC, G, O.

Building Characters from an Exaggerated Trait

Job Interview (My first contact — Second City)

Two players. One player is the interviewer, or "setup player." The interviewer starts the scene by giving a brief pitch about the job. The interviewer's primary objective is to label the applicant by way of the job description, setting him up. The applicant must assume the characteristics of the job, paying off the labels that have been set up for him. As the interviewer asks questions, the applicant adapts to the changing needs of the job and pays off every label in his response. (Focus: developing character point of view, labeling, justifying.) Current usage: Common.

Character from Emotion (My first contact — Viola Spolin's writings)

All players. Players walk randomly around the stage. The instructor calls out a series of emotions. Players feel each emotion, physically and vocally, eventually identifying a word, phrase, or sound that emanates from the emotion and repeating it. (Each player uses a different word.) Next, the instructor calls out an emotion like "forlorn." Players discover an occupation like "Green Grocer." Players assume the character of a green grocer using the specific assigned emotion. The green grocers begin to walk randomly around the stage, speaking the emotional monologue. Players speak about their employment, specific relationships, environment, etc. After players speak simultaneously, the instructor calls on players individually to speak as the character.

> **Forlorn Green Grocer:** *Some of you mangoes have been with us for over three weeks, and your time has come. There's nothing I can do to keep us together. I've washed you, turned you over to keep you from rotting, but there comes a time when you have to say goodbye. Hasta mañana my little yellow amigos.*

(Focus: developing character essence from emotion, discovering character detail from emotion.) Current usage: G.

Panel of Experts (My first contact — LATS)

Four to six players. The instructor assigns an event topic, and assigns one player the role of MC of the event. The remaining players are guest speakers. The MC addresses each player in order. Each player creates a character based on the characters that speak before him. Players can interact with each other while being interviewed and find a game. (Focus: character development, "Yes and.") Current usage: Common.

Who Am I? (My first contact — Viola Spolin's writings)

Three players. Before the improv starts, a player is sent out of the room, and the two remaining players determine who he'll be — a well known celebrity. The two players start a party scene, anticipating the arrival of the celebrity guest, who soon enters. As the scene progresses, the guest player must guess his own identity, listening for clues and adopting the labels. (Note: Players shouldn't give clues that are too heavy handed — the celebrity will guess his own identity too quickly.)

> **Player One:** *Welcome! The Oscar statuette that you won is sitting safely on our mantelpiece.*
> **Player Two:** *Thanks for keeping it for me while I'm on my ranch. After all, I am Clint Eastwood.*
> **Player One:** *Ha ha! You wish you were Clint Eastwood — you're way too European.*

The celebrity guesses his own identity in first person, in the voice of the character. When a character guesses incorrectly, players must justify it. When the player guesses his own identity correctly, the scene is over. (Focus: listening, labeling, new choice, looking for a game.) Current usage: PW, G, O.

Solo Exercise — Characters from People You Know

Your Grade School Teacher (My first contact — Kip King's On-Camera Acting Technique class)
Solo exercise. In this exercise developed at The Groundlings, create a character based on a schoolteacher or coach from your childhood or teen years. (The year is not important.) Select a person with strong character traits, and be engaged in an activity outside the classroom. (Avoid teaching.) Your images and opinions of this person should be easily accessible and should spark an instant character essence. Write a free-form, three-minute monologue. Then, memorize it for a class performance. (Focus: character based on a familiar person, finding a game, character range.) Current usage: Common.

Building Characters from Labels

Ulterior Motives (My first contact — LATS)
Three players. Before the scene, each player is privately assigned an action to perform contingent on another performer's action. Players must remember to create the scene by adding the foundation, becoming emotional, using a strong stage picture, and object work. Players should use labels as a way to goad the target player to perform as desired. (Focus: setting up your partner, labeling, finding a game.) Current usage: IO, G.

Using Characters in Improvised Scenes

Emotional Symphony (My first contact — LATS)
Group. With all players in an arc, the instructor assigns an emotion for each player. The instructor plays "conductor," pointing at one

player at a time. When pointed to, players vocalize and physicalize their emotions in a repeating form, creating a "symphony." The instructor pairs the players, en masse, to create instant short scenes, where each pair creates a mini-scene based on their conflicting emotions. (Focus: practice overlaying an emotion on an interaction.) Current usage: Common.

Five in a Room (My first contact — ImprovOlympic)
Five players. Each player silently enters and exits a given room, one after another. Each player enters for a specific reason, touches one thing in the room, and exits for a reason. The next player to enter must touch all the things the previous player touched and touch one additional object. Each subsequent player must remember and touch all the previously introduced objects, adding new information that supports the previous players' information. Each player should be aware of the type of room they're creating together and further define it. Players must create a character, add object work, validate the stage picture, and even become emotional. No dialogue. (Focus: object work, foundation, environment, "Yes and," justifying.) Current usage: IO, G, O.

Literary Scenes (My first contact — LATS)
Two to four players. With a given author and title, players perform a scene with dialogue appropriate to the genre, add third-person narration in past tense, detail stage directions, and label the other players. "Brock realized the pretty dame seated across from him was a spy. He drank the last of his single malt scotch and said 'You're the best lookin' CIA agent I've ever seen.'" Common authors are Raymond Chandler, Danielle Steele, Sherlock Holmes, F. Scott Fitzgerald. (Focus: rolodexing, labeling, parody.) Current usage: Common.

Entrance from a Specific Place (My first contact — Viola Spolin)
Two players. The players begin a scene with one "ask-for" — a given location from which characters have just come, which affects everything they do. Players set up the scene with a foundation, but allow their "past life" to influence their current actions; e.g., a couple of chefs have just come from a three-week trip to the desert. (Focus: character history.) Current usage: Common.

Ten Minutes to Set Up a Scene (My first contact — University of Illinois, Urbana/Champaign)

Four to five players. With a given "where," the group plans an improv. In a ten-minute rehearsal session, players plan out their characters and a basic dramatic action for their four-minute scene. As with any improv, the players will add incongruent information and make mistakes despite the best efforts at planning. Players must justify and heighten these errors, e.g., if the "attacking pirates" look more like women from a Neil Simon play, incorporate that truth into the scene. (Focus: linking improv to sketch comedy, justifying, transcribing.) Current usage: G, PW, O.

Character Party (My first contact — University of Illinois, Urbana/Champaign)

All players. In this casual exercise at the end of a character class, all players assemble in a room for a real end-of-class party, with a twist. At the instructor's command, all players become a character that they have developed in the class. Characters interact with one another casually and play off of each other's emotions. (Players should concentrate on interacting with one player at a time as they roam through the party.) After five or ten minutes, at the instructor's command, all players become a second character, continuing the party. This exercise works best if players already know each other's characters, jumping into the middle of the conversation, avoiding slow and painstaking introductions. Players are free to become emotional and must be aware of the give and take of conversation. After the players have done their cache of characters, the instructor asks the players to recount interesting interactions, mining the conversations for possible sketches. (Focus: character history, emotions, listening, continuity, character range.) Current usage: Common.

Long Form Preparation Exercises

Hot Spot (My first contact — IO Los Angeles)

Group. Player One stands on the "hot spot" and boldly performs a solo song. A random player (Player Two) thinks of a song that ties in somehow with the current song, e.g., similar lyrics, tempo, songwriter, theme, etc. Player Two claps in, replaces Player One, and performs the new song. Another random player does the same. (Focus: rolodexing, listening, finding a game.) Current usage: Common.

Call and Deliver (My first contact — The Groundlings)
Two players. In this exercise taught by Ted Michaels at The Groundlings, players start a scene, adding foundation as usual. However, as soon as the scene progresses to the point where a player can identify a game, he "calls it," e.g., "We Hamptons playboys are gorgeous, but fiscally inept!" Then, each character sites three examples of spending money frivolously in order to maintain their appearance (preferably in the present), and the scene is over. That's it. Set up the scene, call it, stamp out iterations of the game, and the scene is over. (Focus: exploring, heightening, finding a game.) Current usage: G.

Godot (My first contact — The Empty Stage, Los Angeles)
Two players. This long form exercise was developed by Stan Wells at the Empty Stage and has migrated to The Groundlings. As in Samuel Beckett's play *Waiting for Godot*, nothing happens here except moments between people. No who, what, or where. Players use minimal dialogue, avoid object work, and explore the silence. Players use a box and a chair, like the rock and tree in *Godot*. A lively stage picture helps the scene establish vital information right from the start. Players do not refer to outside world, just these people in this room, talking to one another. Can the players find a game? Can the players connect with each other to find a simple pattern or theme to their relationship without all the usual trappings? (Focus: stage picture, finding a game.) Current usage: ES, G.

Transformations (My first contact — Viola Spolin's writings)
Two or more players. A variation on the Spolin exercise, players start by mirroring each other with a rhythmic sound and movement. Players watch each other, transform the motion into a recognizable action, and develop a scene from it. With the first line,

players must chime in with instant, excessive agreement. (As a variation, everyone can repeat the first line together, confirming the premise.) If the opening isn't complete in its agreement at the outset, players must start over. Once a solid scene is established and nearing maturity, the players find a new repeating motion within the current scene that they can transform into yet another scene. The Empty Stage extended this exercise into a virtuoso one-hour show called "The Transformers" using a freestyle montage of interrelated, morphing scenes. (Focus: listening, "Yes and," group mind, agreement, positive start, exploring and heightening, finding a game.) Current usage: ES, G, O.

Short Scenes — La Ronde Variation
(My first contact — IO Los Angeles)
Group. A variation on Add Info Lineup/Short Scenes, this game is similar to the La Ronde long form game where the new scene always has one character left over from the previous scene — (the same character in a new situation). In this version, two players begin a short scene and set up the foundation, as usual. However, each subsequent pair of players claps in, replacing the current pair, and starts a new scene based on the theme or information established in the previous scene. In other words, each pair is allowed to build only on a situation or theme referenced in a previous scene — sort of a lightning-fast long form montage. (Focus: exploring, heightening, finding a game, extending the game.) Current usage: G, IO, O.

Long Form Structures

Long Form — Famous Artist/Montage
(Variation on a Groundlings exercise)
Group. The instructor designates one player as a popular painter or sculptor, like Picasso. Start a biographical two-person scene loosely based on the painter's life, with some discussion beforehand about where he lives or his current predicament. Initiate new scenes based on the information revealed in the previous scenes. During this long

form, the painter can monologize, narrating future action. Also, two other players can become the painted versions of the writer's life as it appears in his work. The instructor directs the first scenes. Later, all players are allowed to initiate any scene, old or new. (Focus: explore and heighten, give and take.) Currently in use: O.

Long Form — East Coast/West Coast

Group. The instructor splits the players into two groups — the first group performs the first set. The second group performs the second set.

In set number one, a pair of players start as characters from an east coast metropolis, e.g., Boston. They develop the foundation and find a game in their scene. They embody the attributes and mores of the people from that region. After the initial scene, players from the first group initiate montage scenes, keeping the same city as the location. They expand and heighten the established games and themes throughout a twenty-minute long form set. The instructor calls a blackout at his discretion, ending the set.

In set number two, a pair of players start as characters from a west coast city, e.g., San Diego or Los Angeles. They develop the foundation and find a game in their scene (unrelated to the games in the first set). They embody the attributes and mores of the people from the west coast city. After the initial scene, players from the second group initiate montage scenes, keeping the same city as the location. They expand and heighten the established games and themes throughout a twenty-minute long form set. The instructor calls a blackout at his discretion, ending the set.

Finally, at the instructor's call, all players initiate a third and final set of freestyle montage scenes, including both previous sets. Characters and games from both sets interweave. Each of the two worlds allows its games to influence the other. Players explore reasons for migrating, moving, or visiting the other city to assist the integration of games. (Focus: extending the game; initiating new scenes based on previous scenes; building a world of accord, not accuracy; allowing the game to affect other parts of this world.) Current usage: Common.

Great Character Improvs for Use in Sketch Shows

Rant and Rave (My first contact — Kip King's On–Camera
  Acting Technique class)
Two players. In this Groundlings exercise developed by Cathy
Shambley, Player One rants angrily, and Player Two raves
effervescently about a single chosen topic. The instructor is the
conductor, pointing to each player to continue speaking, sometimes
finishing the sentence or the syllable of the previous player. (Focus:
emotion, rolodexing, listening, "Yes and.") Current usage: Common.

Poetry Slam (My first contact — The Groundlings)
Five players. As if performing at a poetry reading, each of the five
assembled players improvises a single, short poem on the same
topic, based on an audience suggestion like "cloning" or "credit
cards." The five players sit and wait for their "turn" at the
microphone. The players create characters spontaneously as they
listen to each other's poems. Players must create contrasting
characters in the moment, exploring and heightening the games
that previous players introduce. (Focus: creating character
essence, character game, character contrast, listening.) Current
usage: G.

Exercises for Writing Character Monologues

Teacher Monologue (My first contact — Kip King's On-Camera
  Acting Technique class)
Solo exercise. Based on the improv exercise, re-create a quirky
teacher or coach you had when you were growing up, capitalize on
his or her traits, multiply them by one hundred, and create a
character. Improvise a monologue, get instructor critiques,
transcribe, and revise. Focus on the character's activity outside the
classroom. Start in the middle of the scene, establish the person to
whom the character is talking, and make it a high-stakes emotional
day. (Focus: character development, character flaw, incorporating
feedback.) Current usage: KK, G.

Characters from Adjective and Occupation — Monologue
  (My first contact — Viola Spolin's writings)
Solo exercise. First, all players walk randomly around the stage. The instructor calls out a series of adjective/occupation combinations, like "meek attorney." All players "take the plunge" into each assigned character that the instructor calls out, performing brief simultaneous speeches. Finally, the instructor assigns each player a distinct combination like "resentful bartender." Improvise the monologue, get instructor critiques, transcribe, and revise. (Focus: developing a character from an attribute.) Current usage: G, O.

Worst Nightmare — Monologue
  (My first contact — The Groundlings)
Solo exercise. Create a character by embodying the worst possible example of a person in a given field. For example, the character is the "Worst Academic Advisor," or the "Most Preoccupied Grocery Checker," or the "Most Defensive Policeman." The moment we see the character, we identify his flaws. Create a high-stakes emotional beginning, with the character transforming or reaching his objective by the end. Improvise the monologue, get instructor critiques, transcribe, and revise. (Focus: heightening, character development, finding a game.) Current usage: G, O.

Internet Character Monologue
  (Variation on a Groundlings exercise)
The instructor assigns you a character you find on an Internet website. Weblogs, or "blogs," often reveal personal information about real people, and are great character starters. Select a character that is opposite your normal nature, e.g., a "Teamster" or a "Raisin Bargaining Coalition Member." Outside of class, use your research to prepare a character and a free-form monologue. Then, in the next class session, you will perform your monologue. Start with the standard approach: rolodex, "take the plunge" into the character essence, develop the foundation, grow the character game, explore the character's history and defense mechanisms,

and transcribe your improv. (Focus: character development, character flaw, finding a game, incorporating instructor feedback.) Current usage: O.

Exercises for Sketch Writing

Two Worlds Collide — Sketch
  (My first contact — Players Workshop)
Three players. Players improvise a scene using the "fish out of water" concept where they place a who, what, or where in its opposite context. For example, players choose a familiar store and place it in an environment where it doesn't fit, e.g., place a full-service liquor bar in the back of a church as a fundraising activity or open a Hoover vacuum store on the moon. (Focus: scene structure, exploring and heightening, finding a game.) Current usage: Common.

Rewrite History — Sketch (My first contact — The Groundlings)
Two to three players. In this sketch exercise taught by Cathy Shambley at The Groundlings, players improvise a famous historical setting or event and develop the behind-the-scenes characters that shaped the outcome, e.g., Hindenburg, Stonehenge, the Titanic, etc. Improvise the scene, get instructor critiques, transcribe, and revise. (Focus: developing a premise that goes beyond the single behind-the-scenes joke. Develop the concept, the structure, *and* the performance elements.) Current usage: G, SNL.

New Service Employee Sketch
  (Variation on a Players Workshop exercise)
Two players. Improvise and write a character sketch where Player One is a new service employee with a history in another discipline. Player Two is a normal customer who enters Player One's absurd world. For example, Player One is a former biological weapons inspector who is now a pastry chef. Justify the character's change in occupation. Improvise the scene, get instructor critiques,

transcribe, and revise. (Focus: character flaw; physical action; developing the concept, the structure, *and* the performance elements.) Current usage: O.

Index

189

About the Author

Bill Lynn, actor and comedy writer, studied in the professional actor training program at the University of Illinois, Urbana/Champaign. He became a company member of *The Great American People Show*, the theater at Lincoln's New Salem in Illinois, performing in award-winning plays drawn from American history. As a company member of The Blind Parrot theater in Chicago, he performed in and co-wrote the original works *Portrait of a Living Newspaper* and *Dedo, The Life of Amadeo Modigliani*. After several years as a technical writer and corporate trainer, he moved to Los Angeles and wrote and performed in student sketch shows at The Second City L.A. and The Groundlings. He appeared in guest spots on Nickelodeon's *Amanda Show*, and in a variety of independent short films and television commercials. He worked as a comedy writer for an independent Hollywood-based marketing firm, and is a member of the Screen Actors Guild (SAG) and the American Federation of Television and Radio Artists (AFTRA).

Order Form

Meriwether Publishing Ltd.
PO Box 7710
Colorado Springs CO 80933-7710
Phone: 800-937-5297 Fax: 719-594-9916
Website: www.meriwether.com

Please send me the following books:

_____ **Improvisation for Actors and Writers**   **$17.95**
#BK-B269
by Bill Lynn foreword by Kip King
A guidebook for improv lessons in comedy

_____ **Truth in Comedy #BK-B164**   **$17.95**
by Charna Halpern, Del Close and Kim "Howard" Johnson
The manual of improvisation

_____ **Group Improvisation #BK-B259**   **$15.95**
by Peter Gwinn with additional material by Charna Halpern
The manual of ensemble improv games

_____ **Comedy Improvisation #BK-B175**   **$14.95**
by Delton T. Horn
Improv structures and exercises for actors

_____ **Acting Games — Improvisations and**   **$16.95**
Exercises #BK-B168
by Marsh Cassady
A textbook of theatre games and improvisations

_____ **Theatre Games for Young Performers**   **$16.95**
#BK-B188
by Maria C. Novelly
Improvisations and exercises for developing acting skills

_____ **The Ultimate Improv Book #BK-B248**   **$16.95**
by Edward J. Nevraumont, Nicholas P. Hanson and Kurt Smeaton
A complete guide to comedy improvisation

These and other fine Meriwether Publishing books are available at your local bookstore or direct from the publisher. Prices subject to change without notice. Check our website or call for current prices.

Name: _____ e-mail: _____

Organization name: _____

Address: _____

City: _____ State: _____

Zip: _____ Phone: _____

❑ **Check enclosed**

❑ **Visa / MasterCard / Discover #** _____

Signature: _____   *Expiration date:* _____ _____
       (required for credit card orders)

Colorado residents: Please add 3% sales tax.
Shipping: Include $3.95 for the first book and 75¢ for each additional book ordered.

❑ *Please send me a copy of your complete catalog of books and plays.*